C000264543

LONDON TRAMCAR
1861–1952

by
R.W. Kidner

COUNTY HALL AND BOADICEA STATUE. LONDON.

THE OAKWOOD PRESS

© Oakwood Press 1992

First published 1951; reprinted with minor additions 1956, 1960, 1964, 1971, 1974, 1976.
Second Enlarged Edition 1992

ISBN 0 85361 433 4

Typeset by Gem Publishing Company, Brightwell, Wallingford, Oxfordshire.

Printed by Alpha Print (Oxford) Ltd, Witney, Oxfordshire.

AUTHOR'S NOTE

Exploring London's tramways in the 1920s was made easy by the avail-ability of a one shilling (5p) ticket giving all-day travel on every LCC line, and almost all the northern 'borough' lines. And exploration it was, for without magazine or books one did not know what an Ilford tram looked like until one actually saw one – and how fascinating all the different liveries were! After 1933 much of the charm was lost, but still a stroll along the Victoria Embankment had plenty of interest, even without the single-deckers, and with all in uniform London Transport livery. Over the years I went as far east as Horns Cross, as far west as Southall, and as far south as Sutton, and have many pleasant memories. The information I gathered has been supplemented by reading the books of others, and I thank them. There are now, some 60 years after my first voyages, many tramway enthusiasts with more knowledge than I ever dreamed of at that time; if any of them should come across errors or omissions, I trust they will be few.   R.W.K.

Title page
An interesting view opposite County Hall about 1922 showing one of the 1915 (T9–158 series) trailer cars (*left*) also a 'C' class. On the bridge can be seen a single-deck car on the Kingsway Subway service.   *Author's Collection*

A London Street Tramways double deck vehicle licence No. 1547 waits at the Highgate West Hill (Swains Lane) terminus to begin its leisurely run into London's Holborn.   *Author's Collection*

Published by
The OAKWOOD PRESS
P.O.Box 122, Headington, Oxford.

Contents

A 'still' from a Lumiere system cine-film of 1896, showing a South London Tramways car in Southwark Bridge Road. It was photographed by Mr Will Davy Senior of Leicester Square, a cinematograph pioneer. *Author's Collection*

G.F. Train's Victoria Street 2-horse tram of 1861, named *The People* seen here fully loaded and causing great interest.   Author's Collection

Chapter One

The Pioneers

The word 'tramway' has always been an imprecise term; in early Victorian days it was used impartially with 'tramroad' to imply a mineral railway of narrow gauge, using either L-shaped plates and flat wheels, or flanged wheels on edge rails. Granite blocks laid to guide horse-carts in some town streets were also so called; some were of considerable length – that in Commercial Road laid in 1829 was two miles long, and in 1832 a granite tramway was proposed from London to Holyhead worked by steam carriages.

Town tramways of the kind this book is about were first seen in America; the New York & Harlem line was opened in 1832, with horse-cars carrying 30 passengers inside and 30 outside on the roof. However, apart from a line at New Orleans, there was no development even in the USA until the 1850s, by which time Paris was proclaiming the merits of city tramways. In 1858 the London Omnibus Tramway Company, under French management, sought unsuccessfully to construct a 'street railway' from Bayswater to Farringdon Street. However, London was a conservative place; the reaction 20 years earlier to the steam omnibuses of Hancock and others had proved that, though in their case there was also the opposition of the horse-dealers.

In 1859 W.J. Curtis, who had inaugurated a line in Liverpool on which cars with flanged wheels and ordinary flat-tyred omnibuses ran together, was given permission to construct a similar line in London, in Islington.

That this was done is vouched for in a letter from its author, W.J. Curtis, to *The Royal Society of Arts Journal* in October 1860: 'The rails are on the ground', said his letter, 'and within a very brief period the public will have an opportunity of judging the value of the system.' But reports in *The Builder* at the time make it almost certain that the line never opened; it is pertinent to recall the words of Sir Benjamin Hall, Chief Commissioner of Public Works, speaking in February 1858 to a deputation in regard to an application to Parliament for tramway powers: 'I have maturely considered the plan, and of all the monstrous propositions which have ever been made or presented to Parliament, this is the worst . . . I shall give the measure my most determined opposition.'

Curtis referred to the flanged-wheel vehicles upon his Liverpool line as 'omnibuses'. In fact the word tram still applied only to such things as colliery tubs.

The tram as we know it was a direct importation from America, brought to our shores by George Francis Train. This flamboyant character had studied street tramways in New York and Paris, and laid a line at Birkenhead. He received grudging permission to lay three short lines in London, and these were opened as follows: from Marble Arch along the Bayswater Road to Notting Hill Gate on 23rd March, 1861; from Broad Sanctuary up Victoria Street to the Vauxhall Bridge Road on 15th April, 1861; and from the east end of Westminster Bridge to Kennington from 15th August, 1861.

It is recorded that George Cruikshank was the first man to ride on a London tramcar, at the opening of the Bayswater line, and that Charles Dickens and Thackeray were also present. The occasion was marked by a banquet, to which President Lincoln and the Duke of Cambridge were

A contemporary print of G.F. Train's Bayswater Road tram of 1861, seen here at Marble Arch. The artist has somewhat exaggerated the size of the vehicle which would have been quite a load for the two horses.

Author's Collection

invited, although they did not attend. The opening of the Victoria Street line was inaugurated by an 'American Breakfast' at the Westminster Palace Hotel. Train intended this line to continue over Westminster Bridge (already laid with granite trams) to join the Kennington line, but the thought of these new-fangled contraptions actually running past the seat of Government could not be tolerated.

The tramcars, which were, of course, hauled by horses, were built upon the American pattern, with some of the opulent vulgarity of early Pullman cars, by Kimball & Bolton of Philadelphia. Contemporary reports refer to the Victoria Street one as a 60-seater, though its length cannot have much exceeded 20 feet. It is more likely that it seated only thirty. The innovation, alas, was short-lived. Two things led to Train's defeat: he was an American, and his lines were dubbed 'Yankee Railroads' to their detriment in the eyes of a very jingoistic public; further, the iron step-rail which he used projected above the roadway, and quickly earned the hostility of the other highway users. Some newspapers were hostile; one even went to the length of calling Train 'a Fenian Brigand' though there is no evidence that he was of Irish descent.

It seems that the step-rail which caused the trouble was used in Philadelphia, where its flat sunken surface enabled horse-carts to use it. A similar rail was laid in the Rhymney Valley in South Wales for a 'railway' opened in 1825, where traps and carts used the rails along with the trains, even after steam-haulage was adopted. However, it was clearly not a suitable kind of track for London.

The Bayswater line was ordered to be closed and removed by 4th October, 1861. Wrote The Engineer: 'Train, with a certain amount of bravado, put his rails down directly under the noses of the wealthy residents of Bayswater, mostly "carriage people", who even if they had no prejudice whatever against tramcars, had little occasion to use them, still less in the direction of Notting Hill.' It will thus be seen that the association with kippers and stale beer which has been the London tram's lot for nearly a century was present at its birth. The journal was good enough to add, 'in its extended trial nobody has been killed'. The removal of the Victoria Street line was ordered by mid-March 1862, and a conviction against Train in respect of the third line was obtained at the Surrey Assizes in April 1862. It is of interest that one of Train's associates was J. Clifton Robinson, later Managing Director of the London United Tramways.

A contemporary sketch of a single-ended horse car of the 1880s.

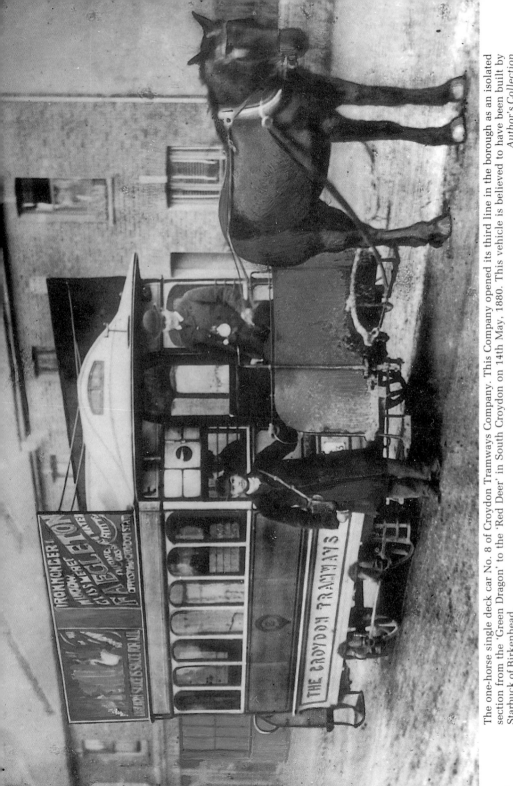

The one-horse single deck car No. 8 of Croydon Tramways Company. This Company opened its third line in the borough as an isolated section from the 'Green Dragon' to the 'Red Deer' in South Croydon on 14th May, 1880. This vehicle is believed to have been built by Starbuck of Birkenhead.

Author's Collection

Chapter Two
A Fresh Start

It must not be supposed that public opinion was solidly against tramways. Schemes continued to be hatched, and in 1865 *The Builder*, discussing plans for new lines, wrote that they would be competitive with the London General Omnibus Company (LGOC) (whose application for tramway powers had failed in 1858). This would constitute a strong recommendation to Londoners, 'who desire to supersede, by an English Company, the French association, which at present overrides the citizens with their bad draughty omnibuses and their broken promises'. It was clear that London, whose population was growing rapidly and pushing up suburbs with great vigour, could not remain tramless for long.

In 1869 Bills were presented by Metropolitan Street Tramways Co., Pimlico Peckham & Greenwich Street Tramways Co. (PP&G), and North Metropolitan Tramways. Before a Parliamentary Committee, experts gave evidence of successful street tramways not only in America but also in Copenhagen and Switzerland. The financial backing for these companies was mainly from the USA, where manufacturers of tramway equipment were eager to assist the London undertakings. The Metropolitan Street line from Kennington Road to Brixton opened on 2nd May, 1870; the PP&G line from New Cross to Blackheath Hill on 13th December, 1870; and the North Metropolitan line from Whitechapel Church to Bow Church on 9th May, 1870.

All the lines operated double-deck cars, with 'knifeboard' seats on top; the North Metropolitan ones were built by Stephenson of New York, and all had a very typical American style, with 7 to 10 small windows having ornate top-lights. The horn-plates were braced across, and braced to the frame corners. The kicking board was in the form of a curved apron, and the horses' haulage straps ran from their collars to the frame corners; shafts were not used, though they had been on the pioneer horse-worked railways, such as the Surrey Iron and Oystermouth. The latter, near Swansea, had by 1858 developed a type of double-deck car quite unlike the American ones; it had started a passenger service in 1807, but as it was classified as a railway, it had never been cited in support of street tramways, notwithstanding the fact that it ran beside a road for its whole length.

In late 1870 the PP&G joined up with the Metropolitan Street Company. The combined concern was titled the London Tramways Company, and became the largest operator south of the river, and one which resisted take-over by the London County Council (LCC) at the end of the century with the greatest vigour. Between 1870 and 1872 the London Tramways line between Vauxhall Bridge and Blackheath Hill was completed, with 25 cars doing seven trips per day, providing a 10-minute service between 8 am and 10 pm. By the end of 1871, 441 cars daily were passing St George's Circus. The tramway era had begun in earnest.

The groove-rail track adopted at this time gave little offence; it comprised a heavy-section rail with the top having a bearing surface for the wheel and a groove in which the wheel flange ran. It was innocuous for horses, though cyclists feared it and some early motor cars with solid tyres found it was best steered over at a wide angle. The almost general choice in London of standard gauge track is perhaps surprising; many undertakings, especially in

A North Metropolitan Tram car No. 217 posing for the cameraman with its two-horse motive power and crew (plus a one eyed passenger) seen here at Clapton in 1879. The line from Moorgate to Clapton was opened in 1873. Note the longitudinal seating on the upper deck.

London Transport

the Midlands and North, opted for 3 ft 6 in. or 4 ft, and there was no apparent advantage in providing the possibility of through running with railways; unlike some European cities, London never had any regular service of rail vehicles working over its tram-tracks. On double-track sections, which later became by far the most common, a 4 ft way was provided against the 6 ft way used on the railways. Tramway vehicles have always been narrower than railway ones; there were a number of places where even this could not be enough, especially on bridges, and 'interlaced' track was then used, providing in effect a single-line section but without the nuisance of points.

The cars used changed little; the first few weighed about 2½ tons empty and ran on 30 inch wheels. The capacity of the horse was a limiting factor; though extra 'chain' or 'trace' horses were put on for some hills, tramcars working over track with grit-filled grooves were always near the limit of capacity of even two horses. It was stated that tram horses had a shorter life than bus horses. The fashion for buying cars from America took some time to die; John Stephenson of New York supplied 221 cars between 1879 and 1883 to the London Tramways Co. and 75 to the North Metropolitan, who soon learnt how to build their own. In view of the simplicity of a horse-tram and the abundance of railway carriage builders, it must appear that 'buying American' was encouraged by the financial managements.

At this point, it may be convenient to consider rapidly the growth of the tramway networks up to the time when the arrival of the electric tram brought about a great change in their fortunes.

The horse-tramway systems of London operated 42 miles of line in 1873, 61 in 1876, and 130 in 1891. In 1891 they carried 200 million passengers, compared with 327 million on the railways and 200 million on the buses. The North Metropolitan Tramways formed the most important single undertaking, with almost 42 miles of route open for traffic in 1891. Its original line of 1870 from Whitechapel to Bow was soon extended into West Ham; it also ran lines in East Ham and Leyton. It covered the whole north and east sector of London from the foot of Highgate Hill to the Docks, a system that required a fleet of 342 cars and 3,346 horses in 1890. The North London (originally North London Suburban) Company was an unsuccessful concern which operated from 1881 until it was taken over by the North Metropolitan in 1891; its lines ran from Stamford Hill through Tottenham to Edmonton and from Finsbury Park to Wood Green. The North Metropolitan's neighbour on the west was a smaller system running from Tottenham Court Road and Gray's Inn Road to Hampstead Heath and the Archway Tavern, called the London Street Tramways; the first portion was opened in 1871, and it had 13½ miles open in 1891, with 124 cars and 1,127 horses.

The remaining tramways north of the Thames were small and isolated; the legislation of the time made it possible for local authorities to veto the laying of tramways, and those of the more prosperous districts, like the City, Westminster, St Marylebone, and Kensington, always did. A cable tramway was opened in 1884 from the Archway Tavern to Southwood Lane, at the top of Highgate Hill. It was closed in 1892 after an accident due to a broken cable and reopened in 1897 (see later).

A former North Metropolitan double-deck horse-tram No. 29 seen here in LCC livery on the Stamford Hill route, photographed *c*.1905. *D.E. Brewster Collection*

LCC horse-tram (licence No. 1472) seen here on the Streatham route (Blackfriars Bridge to Telford Avenue) which included the cable-worked Brixton Hill section. The vehicle appears to be fitted with a slipper brake. *Author's Collection*

The Lea Bridge, Leyton & Walthamstow line was 5 miles long. A stretch from the Lea Bridge to Whipps Cross was opened in 1883, but the company failed soon after; it was not until 1889 that a new company was able to complete the line to Leyton and start running again. The Harrow Road & Paddington was 2.85 miles long, reaching Harlesden in 1888. A branch by the same undertaking along Chippenham Road to Carlton Vale was one of a few 'vanished' tram-routes, having been given up in 1894. The West Metropolitan took over an existing line along the Uxbridge Road at Shepherds Bush and in 1882/3 opened lines to Kew Bridge and Hammersmith Broadway, but had little success until taken over in 1894 by London United Tramways. It also had an isolated section from south of Kew Bridge to Richmond.

The London Tramways Company has already been mentioned; by 1895 there were 24.37 miles open, extending from the south ends of Blackfriars, Westminster and Vauxhall Bridges to Tooting, Streatham, and Greenwich; there was also an isolated section north of Vauxhall Bridge as far as Victoria station. The company owned 287 cars and 3,211 horses, and also operated 37 omnibuses across the bridges it was forbidden to lay its rails on. The section from Kennington Gate to Streatham was converted to cable working in 1893.

To its west was the South London Tramways Co., with routes from HOP Exchange, the Elephant and Castle, and St. Thomas's Hospital to Battersea and Wandsworth, mostly opened in 1884. It operated almost 13 miles, with 86 cars; it also owned 16 omnibuses. The London Southern was a pretentious name for 5¾ miles of line between Vauxhall, Brixton, Camberwell Green, and West Norwood.

The London, Camberwell and Dulwich was a line of 2.87 route miles from Queen's Road, Peckham, to Goose Green and the Plough, Dulwich; these lines were not later electrified. The London, Deptford and Greenwich (the Southwark and Deptford until 1891) was a concern of 6.87 route miles running between Tooley Street, Bricklayers' Arms, and Creek Road, Deptford. The whole of the Tooley Street to Deptford (two thirds of the total) was electrified. Only Bricklayers' Arms to Rotherhithe (one third of the total length) was not electrified, and the last horse tram in London survived on The Rotherhithe Road section until it was closed in 1915. The South-East Metropolitan – another grandiose title – was a cross-line from Greenwich through Lewisham to Catford. The Woolwich and South-East London was a narrow gauge (3 ft 6 in.) line opened on 4th June, 1881 running from the terminus of the London Tramways in Trafalgar Road, Greenwich, through Woolwich to Plumstead; it had 15 cars in 1890.

To the south of London, and not yet connected with its system, the Croydon Tramways Company opened several horse-lines, the first on 9th October, 1879 from Thornton Heath Pond to West Croydon Station; the second line from West Croydon Station to Crown Hill which was opened on 1st January, 1880 and the final section from Green Dragon to 'Red Deer' which opened 14th May, 1880, which was isolated from the other. The Norwood Tramways Company opened two lines in 1883, but later amalgamated with the Croydon Company.

By 1895 the trams had been cut-back to Edmonton (Tramway Avenue) having reached one mile further on at Ponders End, whilst reaching Leytonstone in the north-east, Plumstead, Catford, Dulwich, Streatham, Tooting and Wandsworth in the south, Richmond, Kew Bridge and Acton to the west, and Hampstead and Wood Green in the north. The North Metropolitan Company's covered the largest area and had the longest runs; the lines of the South London and London Deptford & Greenwich were all 4 to 6 miles long; London had two good lines out to Streatham Hill and Tooting; London Street had a tangle of short lines between Euston and Kentish Town, with extensions to Highgate (connecting with the cable tram) and Parliament Hill Fields.

Within 10 years or so these lines would be electrified; what happened to all those horse-trams? Undoubtedly many became garden huts; one was still there 50 years later. One, probably from the last few LCC lines to electrify, was sold in 1912 to the Shropshire & Montgomeryshire Railway, which had a branch with a viaduct that would not take much weight, and was around until 1935; two more, possibly from the narrow gauge line in Woolwich, were bought by the Torrington & Marland Railway in Devon (which also had a weak wooden viaduct) to carry workmen from Torrington station to the china clay mines. Possibly some other uses may have been found, but no doubt most were burned, as their successors were 50 years later.

Tram No. 1 of the South Eastern Metropolitan Tramways. This car was constructed at the works of the North Metropolitan Tramway Co. Note the garden-type seats on the top deck and the decorative cast wheels.   *Courtesy Tramway & Railway World*

Chapter Three
New Motive Power

As can be seen, this complex network of tramways made a heavy call on the supply of horses. The North Metropolitan had hired its horses from the LGOC until 1878, at 6¾d. per car mile, and the London Street Tramways adopted the same system until 1873. Hereafter each company built up its own stables – and they were of considerable size. There had to be eleven horses for every car in service: five pairs to work in shifts, and one horse spare in the stables. A tram-horse's working life was four years – this was six months less than for an omnibus horse; although the trams rolled more readily when in motion, they were heavier and required more effort to start. Stops were more frequent, too: there were, alas, many people who had no compunction in stopping a tram on a sharp rise, when a walk of a few yards would have spared the horses a heavy start.

Steam

London was inclined to be slow off the mark with tramway developments. While a state of masterly inactivity obtained in the capital, provincial towns made the costly and sometimes painful experiments. This was certainly true of the steam tramway locomotive, which was developed in 1876 and tried out in Leicester, Leeds, Newcastle, Glasgow and other cities before its adoption in London in 1885. But the metropolis can boast of an early – if unsuccessful – experiment with a car containing its own steam motive power.

This was a 54-seat double-decker, designed by J. Grantham and built by the Oldbury Carriage & Wagon Co., with Merryweather engine, whose trials took place at midnight of 26th November, 1873 in the Vauxhall Bridge Road. The car was entered at the ends, and there were two boilers, one each side of the gangway in the centre. The two cylinders (4 in. × 10 in.) drove one pair of wheels only, 30 in. in diameter. As designed, the car had four grooved wheels and four road wheels (two driven), but it is doubtful whether it ever ran so fitted. The trials were not entirely successful, due to lack of steam and dirt in the rail grooves. The car was sent to the West London Extension Railway near West Brompton Station, where it ran for a time on exhibition, and then was sold to the newly-opened Wantage Tramway. Here, rebuilt with only one boiler, it gave a good account of itself.

At about the same time, Loftus Perkins tried in London his steam tram-horse; a single large rubber-tyred wheel drove and steered: the two wheels at the rear may have been flanged, but it is not clear in the account. The engine had a vertical boiler and two pairs of compound cylinders driving the wheel through gearing.

Steam tramway locomotives were first used in the UK at Leicester in 1876. In 1879 Parliament applied rigid restrictions; they must not allow escape of steam (therefore condensers were fitted) and all motion must be enclosed by skirting panels. If not fitted with duplicate controls at each end, they must be driven with the boiler to the rear, that is cab foremost; in practice most were double-ended. They were coke-fired to avoid smoke, and were all four-wheeled. If drawing open-topped trailers (which were almost all of the bogie type), the chimney was tall to take cinders clear of the top deck (not

Major Beaumont's compressed-air tramcar 'dummy' No. 2 of 1880 being charged with air (at the front) from a pipe beneath the track at Stratford Broadway. It is coupled to a North Metropolitan double-deck tramcar No. 8 and captured by a contemporary artist for the Illustrated London News.

Author's Collection

A contemporary engraving of J. Grantham's steam tramcar of 1873 which was tried in London in 1874. It is shown here with four rail-wheels and four larger road wheels but it is doubtful whether the latter were ever fitted. This tram later ran on the Wantage Tramway near Didcot (an account of its service is carried in the publication on *The Wantage Tramway* published by the Oakwood Press).

Author's Collection

A Dick Kerr steam driven tram engine No. 18 of North London Tramways photographed here about 1889 with Falcon bogie trailer at Wood Green. Note the roof condenser on the engine. *London Transport*

always successful). Most had horizontal boilers and direct drive, being in effect scaled-down railway engines, but an engineer called Wilkinson patented a tramway engine with vertical boiler and geared drive, which was built by several manufacturers, though none were seen in London. There were 532 tram engines at work in Britain in 1894 and only 25 in London, so the Capital's part in this development was small. It is probably true that if tramway managements had paid more attention to experiments with electric trams, the steam era, which lasted only some 20 years, could have been avoided.

The company which did bring in steam was the North London, in 1885, with 15 engines built by Merryweather working on the Edmonton line, with bogie trailers built by Falcon Engine & Car Works Ltd (successors to the pioneer steam tram builders, Henry Hughes & Co.). In 1886/7 ten engines by Dick, Kerr were added. The records show only 27 trailers cars (built 1884–7) so it appears they worked singly, though there is a photograph of an engine with two. The North London was shaky financially and in 1891 sold out to North London Suburban, who took the steam trams off the road and went back to horse cars. The most probable reason for this would be wear of the track; the Merryweathers were not as heavy as some, being under 8 tons, but like all four-wheelers they would have shimmied along, producing various pressures. They had $7\frac{1}{2}$ in. $\times$ 12 in. cylinders, 2 ft 4 in. wheels and 5 ft wheelbase. The Dick Kerrs, if of standard type, did have 8 in. $\times$ 14 in. cylinders, 2 ft 6 in. driving wheels, and weighed $8\frac{1}{2}$ tons. The overall length was $11\frac{1}{2}$ ft.

Both types had roof condensers with some 400 sq. ft. of surface in the form of tubes the condensate was returned to a tank under the footplate. Running was reckoned to cost about 5d. per mile hauling a 60-seat double deck car. They were found preferable to horse cars in some 50 UK cities, and their failure in London must mainly be put down to the operators' unwillingness to capitalise track improvements. It must also be said that over much of the London tramways system at that time, there was not the same pressure for heavy carrying capacity as there was in a northern mill town.

Two other tramway locomotives were seen in London: a Merryweather on the Wharncliffe National Rifle Association line on Wimbledon Common, one mile long (1877–82); and a Sharp, Stewart working on a line 600 yards long laid experimentally at Buckhurst Hill, Epping Forest, in 1874 by F.H. Trevithick, Engineer of the Lisbon Tramways in Portugal. Curiously, the last tram engines to be seen in the London area were four 'Wilkinsons' from the Plymouth Tramways, which later worked at White's Swanscombe cement works and reportedly lasted until 1924.

Compressed Air

Driving trams by compressed air, using cylinders charged to high pressure at lineside points, was an attractive idea and had some success, though not in London. The most popular system was that of a Frenchman, Mekarski, and cars of his were tried in 1881 on the North Metropolitan and later London Street. A British system was devised by Major Beaumont, an army officer who was enthusiastic for compressed air. He had a 'dummy' (a tram

A drawing of a horse-car seen here converted to battery-traction and running in West London in 1883.   *Author's Collection*

In 1892 The Electric Tramcar Syndicate put two battery-driven Jarman tramcars on the Croydon Company's Thornton Heath line, working in service with the horse drawn vehicles.   *London Transport*

engine not carrying passengers) built and demonstrated at Woolwich Arsenal in 1880, a 0–4–0 of rather crude design. However he also built a second dummy, numbered 2, which 'was intended for the North Metropolitan Tramway' and seems to have run on the Stratford line for some time in 1881 ornately painted and with a bright canvas cover for the driver; it towed a normal North Met 4-wheeled double-deck car. These dummies are believed to have been built by Manning, Wardle of Leeds, though possibly equipped by Greenwood & Batley. No. 1 had six cylinders (three pairs) and No. 2 two pairs.

In 1882 Sir F. Bramwell designed a self-contained compressed-air tram, with two cylinders $5\frac{3}{8}$ in. $\times$ $10\frac{1}{4}$ in. and 450 lb. pressure, to work along the Caledonian Road. It was built, but if it ran its life was brief.

Cable Traction

Cable traction has a long and still continuing history of operating passenger cars on gradients; many short steep 'cliff' lines are still operating, though longer ones, such as the 'Steep Grade' railways at The Dyke and Sandgate failed long ago. In London, it was a subsidiary company of an American concern working the Hallidie patents, the Steep Grade Tramways & Works Co., who brought cable trams to Highgate in 1884, with a three-quarter-mile line having gradients from 1 in 11 to 1 in 15. Bogie cars with knifeboard seats on the roof ran between Archway Tavern and Southwood Lane, powered by a 50 hp engine in Highgate High Street. Following an accident in 1892 the line closed, but was re-opened in 1897 by a different company using four-wheeled cars drawn by 'dummies'. The line was converted to electric traction in 1907.

Another cable-operated line was opened in 1892 to surmount Brixton Hill. However it was not confined to the Hill, but worked the whole line from Kennington to Streatham, part of the London Tramways Co. system. The cable was six miles long, constantly moving at about 8 mph, and 'gripper' dummies hauling horse trams were provided, though later large horse-trams fitted with the gripper gear were substituted. Conversion to electric propulsion came in June 1904.

Storage Battery Cars

But the most attractive siren beckoning to tramway engineers was the electric accumulator. It had everything: there was no noise, no smell; it was suitable for installing in converted horse-cars, and required no alterations to the track. But, alas, this bouncing baby among traction systems was born a heavyweight, and no amount of striving on battery development could make any substantial reduction. Moreover, the charge was good for only 30 miles or so of running, and as time went on it seemed unlikely that this figure could be substantially increased. The first trials were made at Leytonstone on 4th March, 1882 with a horse-car equipped on the Radcliffe-Ward system. A few months later another car equipped by Greenwood & Batley to the design of Mr V.G. Lironi ran for a time between Stratford and Manor Park. A car tried at Kew Bridge in 1883 was of only 6 horse-power. The South London and West Metropolitan Companies also ran trials at this time. In

A commercial postcard view of the loop at the top of the 3 ft 6 in. gauge cable-worked tramway up at Highgate Hill, showing clearly the centre conduit, photographed around 1906. *Author's Collection*

No. 928, a Streatham cable-line passenger-carrying 'gripper' car on Streatham Hill in 1900. Note the reversible seating on the upper deck. *London Transport*

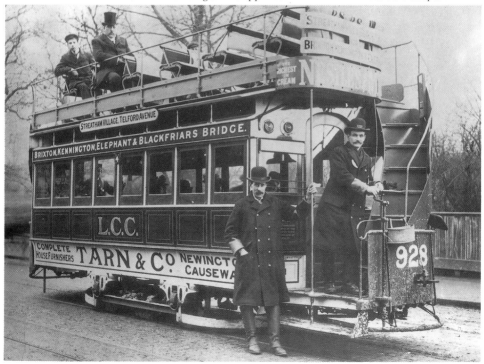

A gripper 'dummy' No. 18 seen here on the Streatham Hill cable-line of the London Tramways Company. These vehicles were withdrawn by the LCCT in 1899.

Author's Collection

A Highgate Hill Tramways Company cable tram 'gripper' car and trailer, almost certainly owned by the Limited company (1897).

London Transport

September 1885 a much-publicised trial was made with a Jarman battery car, weighing 6½ tons, between Blackfriars Bridge and Clapham, taking 29 minutes for the 4 miles on the outward journey and 37 minutes on the return.

Six Eliesons system battery tram engines were run from Manor Park to Stratford Church, on the North Met. between August 1886 and October 1887. Then between 1889 and 1893 the General Electric Power & Traction Company worked the North Metropolitan's Barking Road line with five 52-seat battery cars, for 4½d. per car mile: on withdrawal the cars had run a total of 76,398 miles. Six battery cars were working between Clapham and Tooting in the spring of 1890, and in 1891 Alderman D.B. Miller, Chairman of the Croydon Tramways Company, converted a horse-car to battery traction at Thornton Heath, but withdrew it after trouble due to acid spilling on the journey. However the same company put two Jarman System cars to work on the Thornton Heath line in 1892.

Battery cars cannot have been convenient to run; it was stated of a bogie single-deck car tried on the South London Tramways in Battersea (only at night) that half a ton of batteries had to be run out for recharging at the end of each run. The car itself weighed 4 tons, and the top speed was 6 mph. It was said that the withdrawal of the battery trams by the North Metropolitan was solely due to bad track; however, at a congress of the Tramway & Light Railway Association in 1908, Sir Clifton Robinson stated 'the accumulator system has been dead for years and shows little or no symptoms of resuscitation.'

Internal Combustion

Early petrol engines were not applicable to tramways, because a suitable transmission system had not been invented to take a heavy load. The gas tram, one of which was tried in Croydon, got over this by having a straightforward dog-clutch with an enormous flywheel to absorb the inertia shock. This was housed in a covering at one side of the car; the engine was a two-cylinder horizontally-opposed German Deutz type; the cylinders were of 7½ in. diameter, the flywheel 4½ ft, the gas container measured 25 ft by 4 ft and the weight was 5½ tons. These cars operated for 10 years from 1897 on the Trafford Park Tramway in Lancashire, but not very reliably. They ran on coal gas; earlier a Connelly gas dummy running on oil-gas had been tried, in 1893, between Tooley Street and Deptford, but was not taken on. It also had trials at Croydon and Stratford.

A more suitable system was the petrol-electric, where the engine drove a dynamo which in turn drove motors on the wheels. This was devised by W.A. Stevens of Maidstone, and known first as the Hallford-Stevens and then as the Tilling-Stevens system. There was no need for a clutch or a gearbox, the load take-up being accommodated by altering the relation of shunt to compound windings in the circuit. The LCC adapted three horse cars with this system in 1913, but they worked for only a few months, from May to November; it seems that vibration, noise and smell made them unpopular. It is interesting that 20 years later LPTB was using former Tilling-Stevens buses, of which many hundreds ran in London and the provinces, as tower-wagons for overhead repair.

Chapter Four
Electricity at Last

It is important here to consider the general position of London passenger transport. In the early 1890s there was a fully-developed suburban railway system, but trains were mainly slow and uncomfortable, and often reached a London terminus (itself not necessarily in the centre of the city) by very roundabout routes. The motor bus had not been invented, and if it had been the streets were too badly surfaced to have allowed it to succeed. The capacity of the horse-tram had long ago been reached. Therefore, when experiments with electric tramcars supplied with current from conduits and overhead wires succeeded in Germany, France and N. Ireland, it was certain that the English towns and cities would ultimately follow, in spite of the high capital cost of such installations. A tram had, in fact, been running along the front at Brighton since 1883, though this took current from an open conductor-rail, which was not possible in town streets.

The first electric line in the vicinity of London was opened at Northfleet in March 1889, a short extension of an existing 3 ft 6 in. gauge Gravesend –Northfleet horse line, from a depot in London Road to Station Road. It was sponsored by the Series Electric Traction Syndicate and built by the well-known firm of Dick, Kerr, the cars being built at the Falcon Works at Loughborough, with Elwell-Parker motors. The system comprised a positive and negative cable running in an 8 in. diameter conduit; each car carried a long collector bar which ran inside the conduit, being connected to the car by bars passing through a slot immediately inside one running rail. At regular intervals the supply cable was broken by a pair of plates, held together by springs: these the collector parted, and in so doing connected the motor terminals to the supply and return cables. The collector was of such a length that it was always in contact with one pair of plates. The effect of this system, the wiring diagram of which is too complex to discuss here, was that any number of cars could be run at one time in series. With only one car operating, the drain on the generating plant was 60 amps at 165 volts.

The cars were powered by 15 hp motors geared down at 1:4½. The track was somewhat peculiar, in that the conduit was integral with one of the running lines, the other line being normal tramway groove-rail. Two bull-head rails were laid with a small gap between in which the bar holding the collector ran, the carrying wheels bearing on the outer rail. This was done to avoid having to dig up the road between the tracks, but would have been inconvenient in a complex layout; the electric line did have four passing-places (including termini) and the points operated a moving tongue inside the conduit, which diverted the collector-bar connector to follow the wheels.

It is perhaps no coincidence that a number of pivotal conclusions in London's decision-making circles came together about the turn of the century. The feasibility of electric underground railways was now proved; the ability to run reliable motor bus services was proved by 1904; the practicality of the electric tram could not be ignored after 1901. All these confirmed the death sentence for the horse-tramway. If the tramway undertakings were to survive, they must put themselves in a position to compete; their 'easy ride' against the horse-bus and steam railway was over.

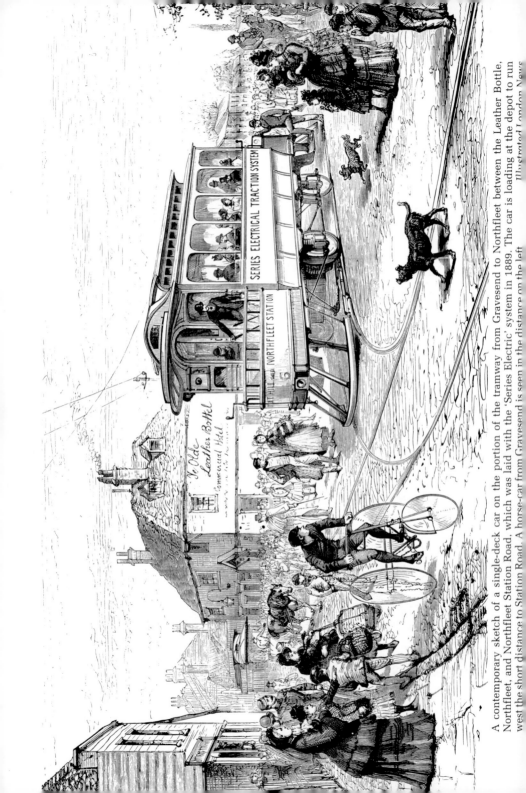

A contemporary sketch of a single-deck car on the portion of the tramway from Gravesend to Northfleet between the Leather Bottle, Northfleet, and Northfleet Station Road, which was laid with the 'Series Electric' system in 1889. The car is loading at the depot to run west the short distance to Station Road. A horse-car from Gravesend is seen in the distance on the left *Illustrated London News*

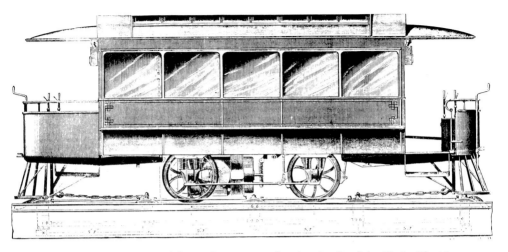

An engraving reproduced from *The Engineer* showing details of the 'Series Electric Car' indicates the full-length electric current collector which ran in a conduit under one of the running rails (*see front view*). *The Engineer*

The first electric overhead tram in Middlesex; a single deck German car on the Alexandra Palace Electric Railway which was laid down in 1898 but removed only a year later. *Author's Collection*

The first town tramway, with overhead pick-up by 'trolley wire', was opened at Roundhay in Leeds in 1891. The first extensive system was at Bristol, opened in October 1895, one of the prime movers being Clifton Robinson, later of London United Tramways. The London County Council did not begin serious discussions until 1898; it was to be five years before the Council's first electrified tramway was working. The delay was not, as is usual, caused by the need to develop the equipment; it was all there in the USA ready to be imported or copied. But there was a snag; the easiest system was the overhead, a boom on the car roof picking up current via a wheel running along a wire, returning to negative via the rails. But even though trams of any sort were banned from inner London, the idea of trolley-wire poles in parts of London several miles out was considered unseemly. Therefore decisions had to be made about the use of conduit pick-up.

There were two forms of conduit: the open, in which a 'plough' attached to the car ran in an open slot, picking up current from a live rail in the conduit; and the closed or surface-contact type. There were several variants of the latter system: in every case the cable was laid in a tube beneath the tracks, and connected to frequent electric studs in the roadway surface, which only became 'live' when a magnetised 'skate' beneath the car ran over them. The overhead trolley was the cheapest system to install, the open conduit costing nearly twice as much, the cost of a closed conduit lying between. The surface-contact in practice proved unpredictable in conditions of dirt and ice; sometimes the studs remained alive after the skate had passed, to the detriment of horse-traffic.

In 1898 a short electric tramway was built at Alexandra Palace, with 600 yards of track, worked by the Wandruszka Electrical Co. of America using four German single-deck cars with trolley pick-up. It was taken up in 1899 but the route was used by a later MET branch.

In outer London things had moved faster; East Ham and Croydon both had electric tramways in 1901. London United had met some difficulties in negotiating with the Middlesex County Council, but was also able to go electric in 1901. All the LCC had was a sample car used in the Camberwell depot to train drivers. But the pace of electrification was gathering everywhere.

It was only just in time; by 1904 the motor-bus had proved itself (although no British manufacturer had yet brought out a satisfactory chassis, there were plenty of French and German ones) and was able to pick up in Central London, which the trams could not, and also penetrate to suburbs that trams had not yet reached. However, the travelling public was increasing rapidly, and there was enough traffic for both. Competition between the LGOC and other bus operators and the trams was fierce, though a few years later when the 'Company' tram fleets and the buses were in common ownership, this was much reduced.

Here mention must be made of the career of a person who played a large part in the introduction of electric trams, Sir Clifton Robinson. He was a native of Birkenhead, and as a boy saw Train's tramway there. He later stated 'I pursued that car, got on to it, held on to it, and from that day to this have never let go of tramways' (in an interview in 1907). He joined Train in

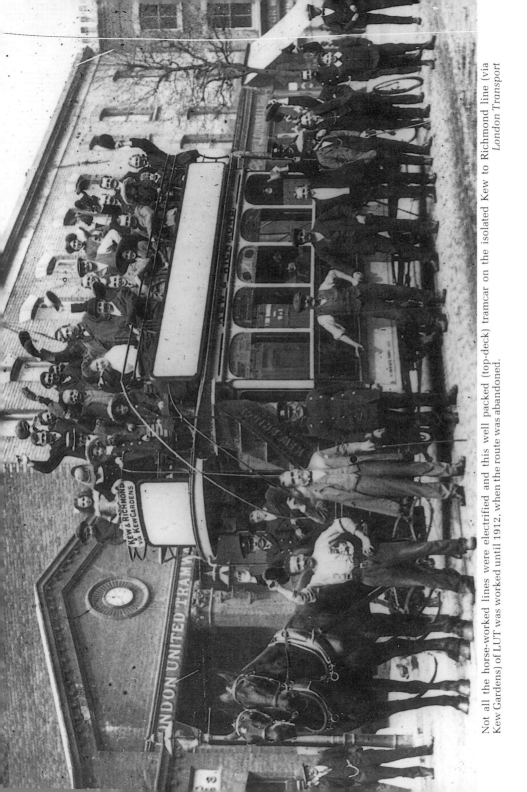

Not all the horse-worked lines were electrified and this well packed (top-deck) tramcar on the isolated Kew to Richmond line (via Kew Gardens) of LUT was worked until 1912, when the route was abandoned.

London Transport

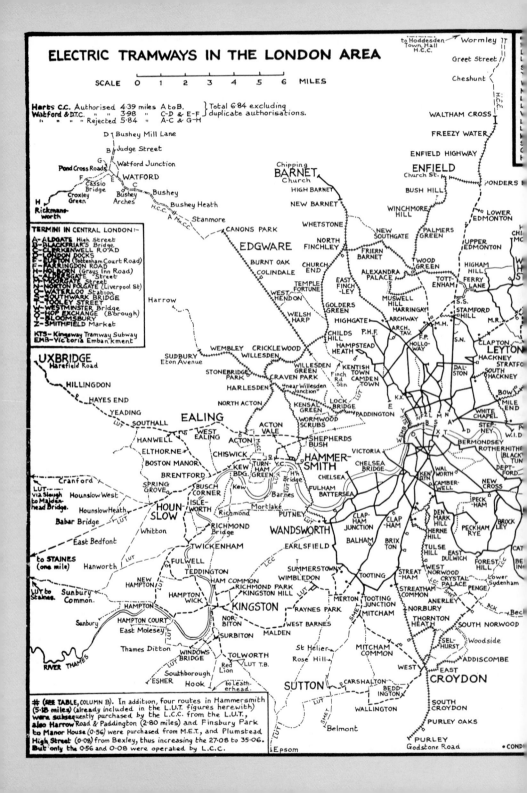

ELECTRIC TRAMWAYS IN THE LONDON AREA

SCALE 0 1 2 3 4 5 6 MILES

Herts C.C. Authorised 4.39 miles A to B.
Watford & D.T.C. " " 3.98 " C-D & E-F
" " " Rejected 5.84 " A-C & G-H

Total 6.84 excluding
duplicate authorisations.

TERMINI IN CENTRAL LONDON:—
A—ALDGATE High Street
B—BLACKFRIAR'S Bridge
C—CLERKENWELL ROAD
D—LONDON DOCKS
E—FARRINGDON (Tottenham Court Road)
F—FARRINGDON ROAD
H—HOLBORN (Grays Inn Road)
J—ALDGATE Street
K—MOORGATE Street
N—NORTON FOLGATE (Liverpool St)
O—WATERLOO Station
S—SOUTHWARK BRIDGE
T—TOLLEY STREET
W—WESTMINSTER Bridge
X—HOP EXCHANGE (B'brough)
Y—BLOOMSBURY
Z—SMITHFIELD Market
KTS—Kingsway Tramway Subway
EMB—Victoria Embankment

(SEE TABLE, COLUMN B). In addition, four routes in Hammersmith
(5.18 miles) (already included in the L.U.T. figures herewith)
were subsequently purchased by the L.C.C. from the L.U.T.,
also Harrow Road & Paddington (2.80 miles) and Finsbury Park
to Manor House (0.56) were purchased from M.E.T., and Plumstead
High Street (0.08) from Bexley, thus increasing the 27.08 to 35.06.
But only the 0.56 and 0.08 were operated by L.C.C.

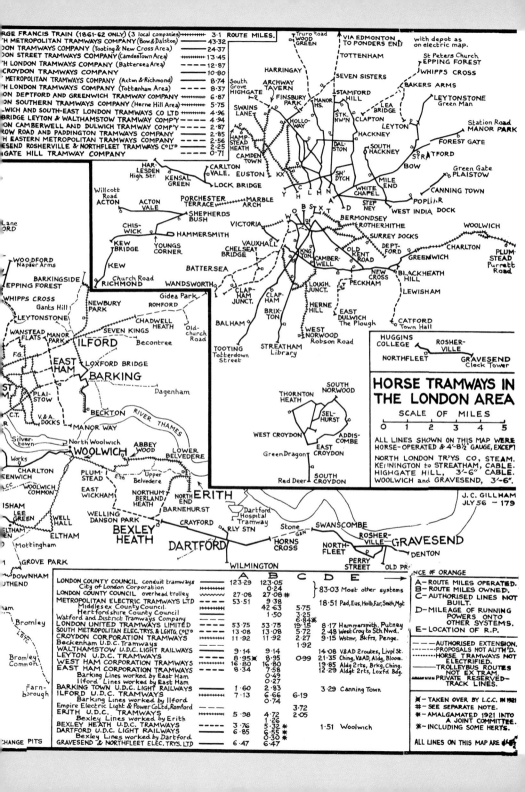

HORSE TRAMWAYS IN THE LONDON AREA

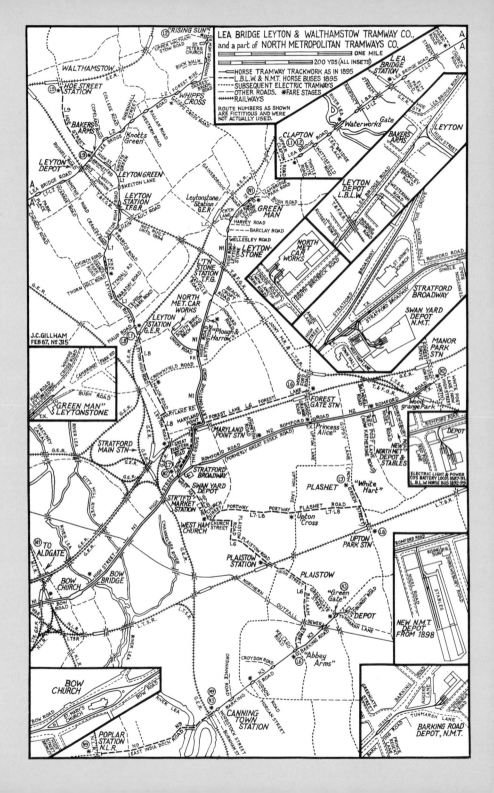

America, came back to work on the Cork Tramways and later in Bristol; then to Edinburgh to set up the cable tramways, which he also did for Highgate Hill. Next it was Los Angeles to get experience of electric trams, and a return to Bristol to join Imperial Tramways in 1891; here the first real electric system of trams opened in 1895. By that time Clifton Robinson was Managing Director and Engineer of London United Tramways.

The London double-deck tramcar went through three phases; open top, covered top with balcony ends, and totally-enclosed top. Stairways were in some cases in two straight sections with a 'landing' in between but more usually of the spiral type and the front shield derived from the horse-cars' kicking board was retained, with a headlight in the centre; a few operators mounted the headlight in front of the top deck, beamed down.

The most important part was of course the 'truck' or trucks on which the body was mounted. This affected how large a body could be fitted, how it would ride, reliability and economy. A favourite four-wheeled truck was the Peckham, which like all other tram components apart from the body hailed from America, though much was manufactured by UK copyists. Edgar Peckham had invented a truck he called a cantilever truck, which was able to adjust to uneven track. It was a built-up truck, and more expensive than the forged ones; after Peckham died in 1920, Brush acquired his rights, though they had been copying the designs for years. The Brush Electrical Engineering Co. Ltd. of Loughborough was by far the largest provider of trucks for Britain. It had by now no connection with Brush of America; one of its founders was Emile Garcke, of BET, and the companies were closely associated. It was able to make controllers and motors, and later the trucks; some work was bought in from firms like British Thomson-Houston. Another very popular four-wheeled truck was the American Brill 21E; this was copied by Brush, Hurst Nelson, and Mountain & Gibson; the J.G. Brill Co., which had a London office, placed advertisements appealing to tramway authorities to only buy 'genuine' Brill trucks, but it had little effect, and trucks recorded as 'Brill' could have been made by several makers or imported from General Electric of America, via their British agents, British Thomson-Houston.

For their bogie trams, all London undertakings used the 'Maximum Traction' type of truck, in which a large pair of wheels took most of the load, the other pair of wheels, called pony wheels, being smaller. Some trucks included a device for transferring weight to the pony axles on curves to obviate any risk of derailment. The design came from Westinghouse of America but was copied by British makers. Brush had a truck of this type designed to be run with the pony wheels outermost, used by the MET, but others used bogies with the traction wheels outermost. Another truck used in London, very similar, was the McGuire, also American. A McGuire factory was set up in Bury, but had to sell out to Mountain & Gibson.

Tramway engineers gave considerable thought to designing a 'radial' four-wheeled truck of extended wheelbase, which would enable a longer body to be fitted and still be easy on curves. The 'radial' action was supposed to give the axles some independence on curved track. Brush supplied a radial, the P35; another one, the Lycett & Conaty, was designed by two municipal tramway engineers, and advertised by Brush and others. It could take a body

LCCT No. 366 (Waterloo Bridge via Old Kent Road) appears to be held up by the horse dray whilst No. 202 passes by.   *Lens of Sutton*

A typical busy early electric tramcar scene at Shepherds Bush Station on the Central London Railway. A London United Z class car No. 63 is heading for Brentford and that on the other line for Ealing, with two cars behind at the terminus. Both these lines were opened in 1901.   *Lens of Sutton*

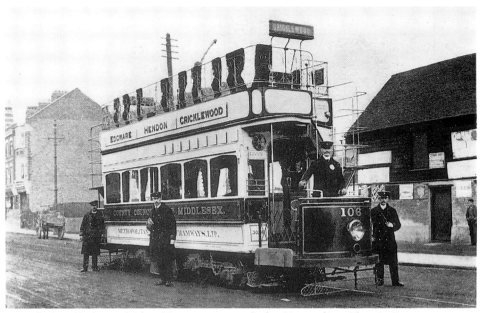

In its 'A' class vehicles (No. 106 portrayed) the Metropolitan Electric Tramways elected to use the type of maximum traction bogie with the pony wheels outer. The route from the 'Crown' at Cricklewood to Edgware opened in 1904. *Lens of Sutton*

The West Ham Corporation's line from Stratford to Plaistow was opened on 27th February, 1904, though Stratford had seen its first horse-tram in 1871. This local commemorative card was issued after the event. *Lens of Sutton*

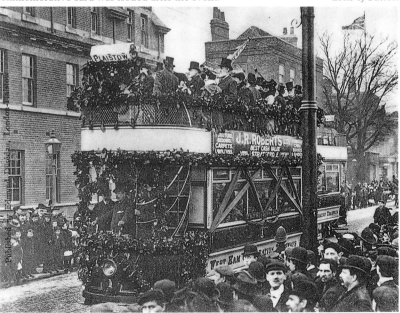

seating 70 passengers, more than some bogie cars. Mountain & Gibson produced their own radial truck, which looked very much like a copy of the Conaty. However, the popularity of radials waned, as it was found that the flexing mechanism did not work very well except when the truck was new.

Many late four-wheeled cars (1911 and after) were built on Peckham 'Pendulum' trucks; this enabled the axles to move laterally and reduced track wear as well as giving a better ride. These were made by several manufacturers, including Brush of course. The identifying of what trucks London trams used is fraught with difficulty, and the information on the tables of stock on a later page must be taken with that in mind. However anyone wishing to study further could not do better than obtain a copy of J.H. Price's Walter Gratwicke Memorial Lecture in 1975 before the Tramway & Light Railway Society, 'The Brush Electrical Co. Ltd.'.

Both the Board of Trade and the Metropolitan Police exercised a rigid control over the design of trams; the latter had been granted powers in 1853 over all types of 'Stage Carriages' and each tram carried a license number by the steps. Operators were required to paint each car every year, and give them a complete overhaul every two. The Board of Trade from the start insisted upon life-guards at each end for scooping up pedestrians; the Company cars mostly had life-guards between the bogies, principally to stop dogs running underneath. The LCC could not do this as it would interfere with the working of the 'plough'.

Safety was always in the minds also of the managements. Braking was important; to supplement the wheel brakes, slipper brakes acting against the rails were brought in, and later made to work magnetically. The LCC had two serious hills, Highgate and Dog Kennel (East Dulwich); here a cam device was used to give extra force to the slipper brake, and the latter hill was four-tracked in 1912 to improve safety.

No precautions could cover every eventuality. The LCC had a serious accident on Eltham Hill in 1928 when two cars collided in such a way as to cut out the magnetic brakes. It was also at Eltham that the perils of 'propelling' were spelt out. Car No. 1103 had failed, and car 988 was attached to its rear by a tow-chain, to propel it to New Cross. A sudden braking by the rear car caused the tow to snap, and the front car, being under hand-brake only, ran away and turned over at a junction.

However, the most spectacular such accident in London was on Archway Road Highgate (not to be confused with Highgate Hill, still at that time cable-worked). MET 'A' class No. 115 ran away and hit a hearse, a furniture van and a bus before colliding with another tram; three people died in this pile-up, on 2nd June, 1906. Fortunately, thanks to competent driving and full sand-boxes, such events were rare.

The next chapter will reveal the curious shape of the London tram boundaries. The LCC was in solid possession of an area from Abbey Wood in Kent across to Wandsworth and northwards to Hampstead, while the Companies had the western and north-western suburbs. In the north-east there was a tight mass of Municipal lines, where each council planned to have its own tramway system within its boundaries. These made little sense, as they were drawn long before trams were thought of, and services could only be made to

work by some inter-running, and the solemn purchase by a council of a few yards of another one's track.

During World War I women drivers and conductors were used to some extent; they were rumoured to be less skilful. A driver on the Gravesend trams, where women were only allowed to drive on the branch lines, told Mr Eric Fayne that the motors of the two demi-cars had been ruined by their driving methods.

The LCC purchased a bogie car from British Westinghouse in 1900 to train drivers being based at the Camberwell depot. It was numbered 101 but renumbered later to 110.   *Cassier's Magazine*

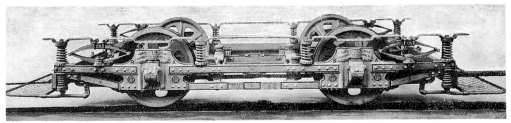

An American Peckham standard car truck as modified for British use with 'life-guards' at either end. The design was copied by British manufacturers, but using forged instead of built-up frames; as also was the similar American Brill 21E truck.
Author's Collection

The LCC 'B' class tram was mounted on Brill 21E trucks; they were built in 1905 and began to be converted to receive top covers in 1906. This vehicle's destination board reads ASYLUM ROAD AND SOUTHWARK BRIDGE VIA OLD KENT ROAD.

London Transport

Chapter Five
The London County Council Tramways

The Tramways Act of 1870 gave powers to local authorities to purchase tramways after a period of 21 years, but this did not apply to lines laid before 1870. The LCC decided in 1891 to exercise its option in all cases, and to consider the matter of the pre-1870 lines; the position was that some companies had lines in both categories. It did not receive powers actually to operate tramways until 1896, and even then this power was not taken up, and when the North Metropolitan was taken over in that year, it had to be leased back for operating.

By 1899 almost all lines within the County had been taken over, and the work began of making them into a whole entity. There had already been some rationalisation, and only twelve companies were involved, North Metropolitan, London Tramways and London Street supplying most of the mileage. Some bits and pieces came later; the Highgate Hill Tramway was not taken until 1909. In the clearing up operation some sections of the North Metropolitan and West Metropolitan which were inside the LCC boundary were electrified by the MET and LUT respectively and acquired by LCCT later; various running rights were also secured.

The first line to be electrified, on 15th May, 1903, was a group from Westminster Bridge (Belvedere Road) to Tooting (Totterdown Street) via Kennington, Clapham and Balham; and from Blackfriars (Stamford Street) to Kennington via St. George's Circus and the Elephant. Conversion continued rapidly until 1910 and thereafter a number of newly-constructed lines were opened, up to 1932. Not all the horse lines were electrified; those left included that from Bricklayers Arms to Rotherhithe, from Old Kent Road Canal Bridge to Rotherhithe, and in Powis Street Woolwich. Horse trams continued to run on the first-mentioned line until 1915.

For the LCC, electrification raised problems which did not arise with some outer London systems, with single track and passing loops with spring-loaded points always set for the left-hand road. The LCC had many multiple junctions, where constructing the conduit was itself a major work; and sometimes pointsmen had not only to set the right road, but if on the 'overhead' part, also set the frog to guide the trolley wheel correctly. There was also the matter of change-points. As the system spread further out to areas where overhead was allowed, provision had to be made for the switch from the conduit. At such places there was a small island between the tracks, inhabited by a skilled tramwayman who wielded the long fork which assisted the 'plough' out of the tram and into a siding of the conduit rail as the car moved slowly forward. The job of switching controls for the new supply, raising the boom at the right time, and getting the plough out without trouble called for teamwork between driver, conductor and change-man. Some cars had two booms, one facing each way; if there was only one boom, it might have to be 'run round'.

There were change-points at Woolwich, Lee Green, Downham (after 1926), Coldharbour (Brixton), Camberwell Green, Streatham High Street, Longley Road (Tooting), Summerstown (from 1931), Putney Bridge Road, Mile End, Iron Bridge (Canning Town), Hackney, Clapton Road, Stamford Hill, Manor House (two), Archway (Highgate), Tooting Junction Station and

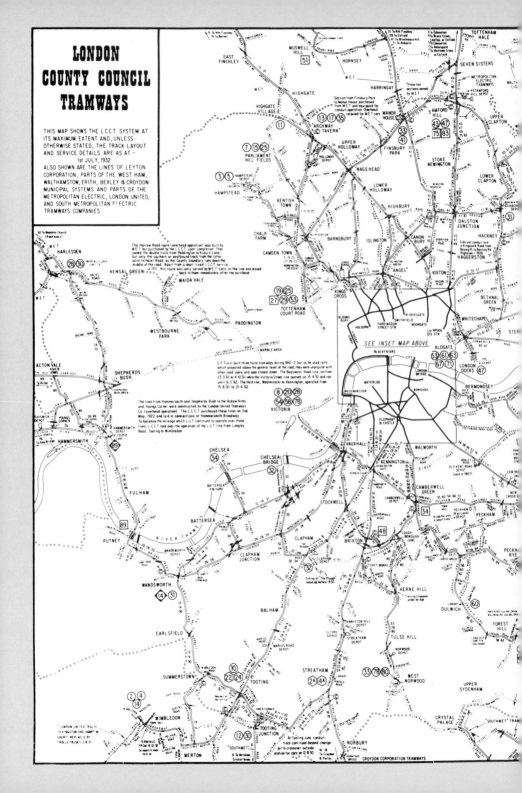

LONDON COUNTY COUNCIL TRAMWAYS

THIS MAP SHOWS THE L.C.C.T. SYSTEM AT ITS MAXIMUM EXTENT AND, UNLESS OTHERWISE STATED, THE TRACK LAYOUT AND SERVICE DETAILS ARE AS AT –
1st JULY, 1932
ALSO SHOWN ARE THE LINES OF LEYTON CORPORATION, PARTS OF THE WEST HAM, WALTHAMSTOW, ERITH, BEXLEY & CROYDON MUNICIPAL SYSTEMS AND PARTS OF THE METROPOLITAN ELECTRIC, LONDON UNITED, AND SOUTH METROPOLITAN ELECTRIC TRAMWAYS COMPANIES

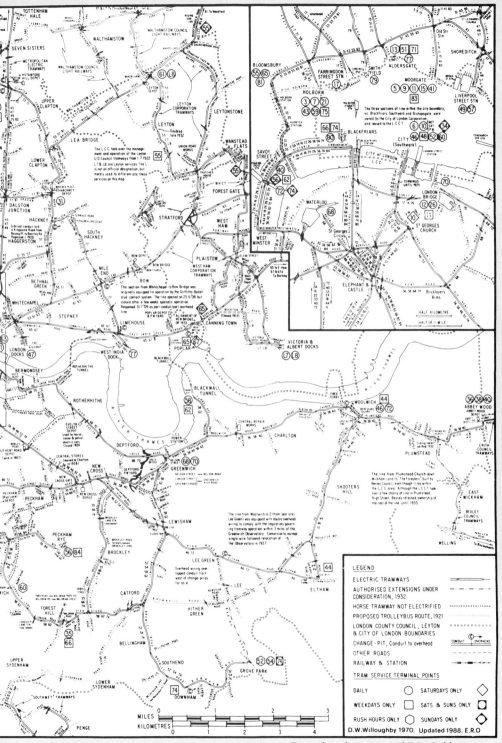

Reproduced courtesy of E.R. Oakley

'A' class tramcar No. 42, on route No. 38, halts in 1931 on the Embankment, seen here at Westminster Pier with New Scotland Yard in the background. It is shown here in its final construction with a complete top-cover. The destination is far-off Abbey Wood. Note the advertisement on the side for cheap mid-day fares from the Embankment, Victoria or City. *Author*

This 'D' class LCC car seen here in 1906 has just been fitted with a top cover with open balconies at each end. They were later enclosed, and Nos. 377–401 which were top-covered later received totally enclosed ones. *London Transport*

The old and the new! An obviously posed photograph of a new LCC 'A' class bogie car No. 50 and a horse tram possibly photographed when the Westminster Bridge to Balham line was opened on 15th May, 1903.   *London Transport*

A busy scene on route 47 from Stamford Hill about 1908, with two horse buses and an 'E' type LCCT tram No. 687. The somewhat general destination on the blind of 'London Docks' refers to Leman Street, near Aldgate.   *D.E. Brewster Collection*

Burdett Road, Limehouse. Some of these were occasioned by through running agreements.

The LCC owned all tramways within its boundaries, but a few stretches were not worked by it. The termini were at Tooley Street; Hop Exchange and London Bridge, for the Borough; north end of Southwark Bridge for the City; Embankment; Victoria; Chelsea Bridge (south end) and Chelsea, Kings Road; Tottenham Court Road (Euston Road); Bloomsbury and Holborn (Gray's Inn Road); Farringdon Street, Smithfield, Aldersgate, Moorgate, Liverpool Street Station and Aldgate. The lines ran out to the County boundaries at Abbey Wood (for the Erith system); Eltham; to join the Bexley system at Plumstead; Grove Park and Forest Hill; Norbury, to join the Croydon lines; Tooting Junction, to join the South Metropolitan Electric Tramways (SMET); Longley Road in Merton, to join the London United Tramways (LUT); Hampstead Heath and Parliament Hill Fields; and junctions were made with the Metropolitan Electric Tramways (MET) at Harlesden, Archway Road, Manor House, and Stamford Hill; connection was made with the Leyton line at Lea Bridge and with West Ham at Bow Bridge and Iron Bridge, East India Docks. In 1932 the LCCT had 167 route miles, including the Leyton system then operated by them.

Through cars ran over MET metals to Barnet, Edmonton, Enfield, and occasionally Wembley and Sudbury; over the LUT to Wimbledon, Acton, Kew Bridge and (summer) Hampton Court; over the Croydon Corporation line to Purley; and over Leyton metals to Bakers Arms, and on Sundays to the Rising Sun. In the other S.W. Essex boroughs the through workings were complex between West Ham, East Ham, Leyton and Walthamstow.

There was at first no connection between the LCCT lines north and south of the river: car movement required fairly complex running over 'foreign' lines. Plans were made for a link-up via a tramway tunnel to be constructed between the projected Embankment line at Waterloo Bridge and the Theobalds Road line (then horse-worked by the North Metropolitan), with a new stretch to be built along Rosebery Avenue to the Angel. This tunnel was opened with clearances for single-deck cars only, on 24th February, 1906 from the north end to Aldwych tram-station. The lower portion below Aldwych was used as a repair depot until the completion of the Embankment Westminster Bridge-Blackfriars Bridge link enabled it to be opened throughout on 10th April, 1908. The tunnel was closed on 2nd February, 1930 and re-opened with clearances for double-deck cars on 14th January, 1931. The length was 3,500 ft and the maximum gradient 1 in 10.

All the early electrification was on the open conduit system; but owing to the great expense involved a section on the Council began to press the claims of the surface-contact system, in particular that of Griffiths & Bedell. The whole thing rapidly became riddled with party politics, the Progressives favouring the conduit and the Moderates the GB. A trial GB surface-contact line was put into operation in 1908 between Aldgate and Bow, and the battle was fought out in the Council Chamber, in an atmosphere far from calm. The GB lost, and the trial line was converted to conduit in 1909; but the feud took some time to die down, the GB patentees having begun a libel action in which it was alleged that LCC engineers had altered the system detrimentally in the course of installation.

A fine side view of No. 733, a 'E' class car which were mounted on Maximum Traction bogies of the McGuire type, manufactured by Mountain & Gibson, to special LCC requirements. In this view the rear bogie is carrying the plough guide. It was photographed before route numbers were adopted in 1912. The three lights above the destination blind (HIGHGATE) indicated the route by a combination of colours.

D.E. Brewster Collection

A 'G' class type single-deck tram No. 599 built for use in the Kingsway subway during the time (February 1906 to April 1908) when Aldwych was as far down the tunnel as the service went. *D.E. Brewster Collection*

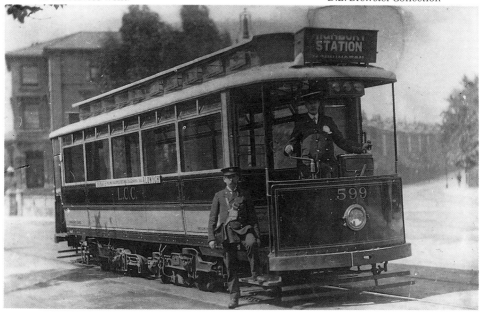

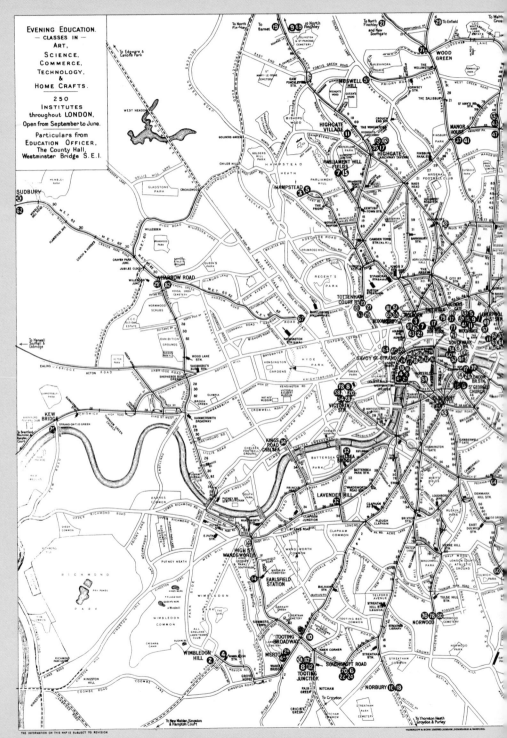

The network as in November 1924.

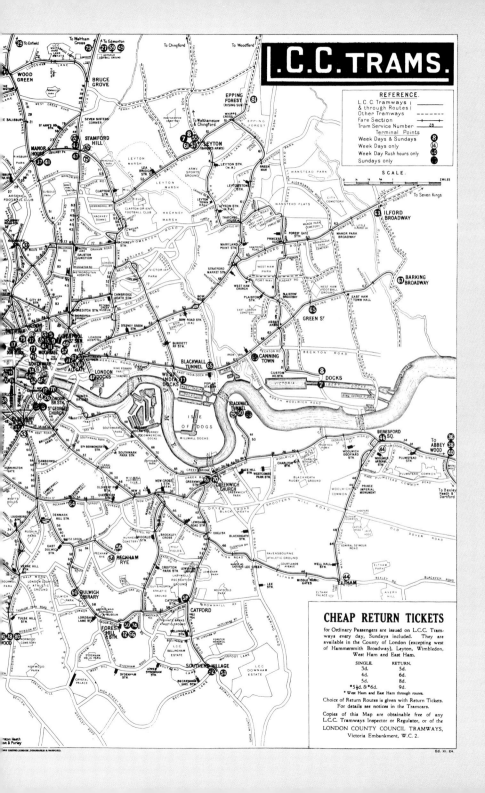

.L.C.C. TRAMS.

REFERENCE.

L.C.C. Tramways	
& through Routes	———
Other Tramways	– – – –
Fare Section	
Tram Service Number	28
Terminal Points	
Week Days & Sundays	8
Week Days only	14
Week Day Rush hours only	60
Sundays only	19

SCALE.

CHEAP RETURN TICKETS

for Ordinary Passengers are issued on L.C.C. Tramways every day, Sundays included. They are available in the County of London (excepting west of Hammersmith Broadway, Leyton, West Ham and East Ham.

SINGLE.	RETURN.
3d.	5d.
4d.	6d.
5d.	8d.
*5½d. & *6d.	9d.

* West Ham and East Ham through routes.

Choice of Return Routes is given with Return Tickets. For details see notices in the Tramcars.

Copies of this Map are obtainable free of any L.C.C. Tramways Inspector or Regulator, or of the LONDON COUNTY COUNCIL TRAMWAYS, Victoria Embankment, W.C. 2.

Ed. XI. 24.

MAP & GUIDE

L.C.C. TRAMS.

NOVEMBER
1924

Victoria Embankment,
W.C. 2.

A. L. C. FELL,
General Manager.

(22,564—10/24.)

ALL-NIGHT SERVICES.

Saturday Nights Excepted.

BATTERSEA (Prince's Head) and BLACKFRIARS (via Vauxhall and Westminster)—

Prince's Head	...	...	...	...	dep. a.m.	12 55, 2 0, 3 0, 4 0
Blackfriars	...	...	...	...	dep. a.m.	1 30, 2 30, 3 30, 4 32

BRIXTON (Water Lane) & VICTORIA EMBANKMENT.
Water Lane via Westminster ... dep. a.m. 1 8, 1 37, 1 53, 2 53, 3 2,
4 56. From Telford Avenue 12 5, 12 34, 3 35
Westminster Station via Blackfriars ... dep. a.m. 12 55, 1 2, 1 30, 1 59,
To Telford Avenue 2 27, 2 55, 3 24, 3 52, 4 21, 5 18, 5 48,
To Brixton Station only, 4 57

CATFORD (St. Laurence's Church) and SAVOY STREET, STRAND (via Old Kent Road and Blackfriars)—
St. Laurence's Church ... dep. a.m. 1 12, thence half-hourly until 4 42 a.m.
Additional cars from New Cross Gate 12 0, 12 30, 1 0
Savoy Street, Strand ... ... dep. a.m. 12 27 thence half-hourly until 3 57 a.m.
To New Cross Gate only, 4 27, 5 0, 5 27

NEW CROSS GATE and SAVOY STREET, STRAND (via Walworth Road and Blackfriars)—
New Cross Gate ... ... dep. a.m. 12 15, thence half-hourly until 4 45
Savoy Street, Strand ... ... dep. a.m. 12 45, " " 5 15

TOOTING BROADWAY and VICTORIA EMBANKMENT.
Tooting via Blackfriars... ... dep. a.m. 12 36, 12 54, 1 27, 1 51, 2 19, 2 48.
Additional Car from Plough, Clapham, at 12 12 a.m.
Blackfriars via Westminster ... dep. a.m. 12 38, 1 6, 1 34, 2 5, 2 31, 2 59
3 28. To Plough, Clapham, only—3 56, 4 25, 4 52

HAMPSTEAD and HOLBORN (via Gt. College Street and Grays Inn Road)—
Hampstead ... ... dep. a.m. 12 18, 1 19, 2 19, 3 25, 4 25
Holborn ... ... dep. a.m. 12 49, 1 49, 2 49, 3 55, 4 55

HIGHGATE and BLOOMSBURY (via Upper Street and Rosebery Avenue)—
Highgate ... ... dep. a.m. 12 27, thence hourly until 4 27
Bloomsbury ... ... dep. a.m. 12 55, " " 4 55

POPLAR and BLOOMSBURY (via Commercial Road and Old Street)—
Poplar ... ... dep. a.m. 12 10, 1 10, 1 40, 2 40, 3 5, 4 17, 4 40
Bloomsbury ... ... dep. a.m. 12 54, 1 54, 2 24, 3 24, 3 54, 4 54, 5 24

STAMFORD HILL and HOLBORN (via Shoreditch)—
Stamford Hill ... ... dep. a.m. 12 30, 1 0, 1 30, 2 0, 2 30, 3 0, 3 30, 4 0
Holborn... ... ... dep. a.m. 1 0, 1 30, 2 0, 2 30, 3 0, 3 31, 4 0, 4 30

THROUGH SERVICES.—The following services are run in conjunction with the authorities named.
9, 19, 21, 27, 28, 30, 48, 51, 55, 59, 71, 79 Metropolitan Electric Tramways Ltd.
7, 8 (Leyton and West Ham) 61, 65, West Ham Corporation.
63, 67, West Ham and East Ham Corporations.
2, 4, 26 London United Tramways Ltd.

The information in the above Time Tables is subject to Revision from time to time.

Copies of this Tramways Map and Guide may be obtained, FREE, of any L.C.C. Tramway Inspector or Regulator; or of—
L.C.C. TRAMWAYS,
VICTORIA EMBANKMENT, W.C. 2,

They are also distributed, to applicants, at the public libraries and many clubs and business houses, supplies to which will be sent on request.

W. & S. LTD.

FIRST AND LAST CARS.
NORTHERN SECTION

3 HAMPSTEAD—HOLBORN
Via Southampton Road, Malden Road, Prince of Wales Road, Great College Street, Pancras Road, King's Cross and Gray's Inn Road

	WEEKDAYS First Car	Last Car	SUNDAYS First Car	Last Car
From HAMPSTEAD	5 21, 5 42	11 38	8 29	11 24
HOLBORN	5 45, 6 12	12 32	8 54	12 0

5 HAMPSTEAD—MOORGATE
Via Southampton Road, Malden Road, Chalk Farm Road, Camden Town, High Street, Crowndale Road, Pancras Road, King's Cross, Pentonville Road, The Angel (Islington) and City Road

	WEEKDAYS First Car	Last Car	SUNDAYS First Car	Last Car
From HAMPSTEAD	4 52	11 30	8 2	11 24
MOORGATE	5 27	12 5	8 52	12 0

7 PARLIAMENT HILL FIELDS—HOLBORN
Via Highgate Road, Kentish Town Road, Great College Street, Pancras Road, King's Cross and Gray's Inn Road

	WEEKDAYS First Car	Last Car	SUNDAYS First Car	Last Car
From PARLIAMENT HILL FIELDS	5 58, 5 30	11 50	8 55	11 44
HOLBORN	6 7	12 16	9 19	12 12

" to Kentish Town Road.

9 NORTH FINCHLEY (TALLY HO CORNER)—MOORGATE
Via Great North Road, Archway Road, Holloway Road, Upper Street, The Angel (Islington) and City Road

	WEEKDAYS First Car	Last Car	SUNDAYS First Car	Last Car
From TALLY HO CORNER	5 45, *5 0	11 38	8 23, *6 8	11 42
MOORGATE	5 28, *5 18	12 14	8 29	11 46
		19 32	7 35	12 34

* From Archway Tavern.
" to Archway Tavern.

11 HIGHGATE VILLAGE—MOORGATE
Via Highgate Hill, Holloway Road, Canonbury Road, New North Road

	WEEKDAYS First Car	Last Car	SUNDAYS First Car	Last Car
From HIGHGATE VILLAGE	7 35, *5 30	11 18	7 53	11 42
MOORGATE	5 58	11 25	8 30	11 46
		19 32	9 35	12 16

* From Archway Tavern.

13 HIGHGATE (ARCHWAY TAVERN)—ALDERSGATE
Via Holloway Road, Upper Street, The Angel (Islington) and Goswell Road

	WEEKDAYS First Car	Last Car
From ARCHWAY TAVERN	4 19	11 13
ALDERSGATE	4 54	11 40

Weekdays only.

Aldersgate Tavern to Smithfield 3 19 & 3 49 only.
Smithfield to Archway Tavern 3 49 & 4 19 only.

15 PARLIAMENT HILL FIELDS—MOORGATE
Via Highgate Road, Kentish Town Road, Great College Street, Pancras Road, Pentonville Road, The Angel (Islington) and City Road

	WEEKDAYS First Car	Last Car	SUNDAYS First Car	Last Car
From PARLIAMENT HILL FIELDS	6 28	11 35	9 0	11 29
MOORGATE	7 3	11 53	9 29	12 4

" to Camden Town Stn.

17 HIGHGATE (ARCHWAY TAVERN)—FARRINGDON STREET STATION
Via Holloway Road, Caledonian Road, King's Cross and Farringdon Road

	WEEKDAYS First Car	Last Car	SUNDAYS First Car	Last Car
From ARCHWAY TAVERN	5 8	11 44	7 15	12 0
FARRINGDON STREET STATION	5 30	12 16	7 44	12 26

19 BARNET—TOTTENHAM COURT ROAD
Via Whetstone, North Finchley, Great North Road, Archway Road, Junction Road, Fortess Road, Kentish Town, Camden Town, High Street and Hampstead Road

	WEEKDAYS First Car	Last Car	SUNDAYS First Car	Last Car
From BARNET	5 4, *4 38	10 54	9 7	10 49
TOTTENHAM COURT ROAD	5 22, *5 29	10 51	8 47, *8 49	10 43
		12 36	8 47, *8 49	10 49

* to Tally Ho.
" From Tally Ho.
Sundays—Early Cars Highgate to Tottenham Court Road 7.42 to 8.18

---

21 NORTH FINCHLEY (TALLY HO CORNER)—HOLBORN
Via New Southgate, Bounds Green Road, Wood Green, Harringay, Finsbury Park, Seven Sisters Road, Caledonian Road, King's Cross and Gray's Inn Road

	WEEKDAYS First Car	Last Car	SUNDAYS First Car	Last Car
From TALLY HO CORNER	6 16, *3 22	10 28	*8 51	12 15
HOLBORN			*8 51	12 15
to Finsbury Park	3 16		*8 34	11 28
HOLBORN	3 56, 4 48, 7 20	11 10	*8 34	
to Finsbury Park	3 56, 4 48	11 30		

* From Finsbury Park. 7 20 (Wood Green).

27 EDMONTON (TOWN HALL)—TOTTENHAM COURT ROAD
Via Tottenham, High Road, Seven Sisters Road, Parkhurst Road, Camden Town, Camden Town, High Street and Hampstead Road

	WEEKDAYS First Car	Last Car	SUNDAYS First Car	Last Car
From EDMONTON (Town Hall)	6 38	6 59	9 32	11 6
TOTTENHAM COURT ROAD	7 31, *6 2	7 44	10 20, *9 59	11 6

to Nag's Head, Holloway.
(to Nag's Head 12 31)

29 ENFIELD—TOTTENHAM COURT ROAD
Via Palmers Green, Wood Green, Harringay, Finsbury Park, Seven Sisters Road, Parkhurst Road, Camden Town, Camden Town, High Street and Hampstead Road

	WEEKDAYS First Car	Last Car	SUNDAYS First Car	Last Car
From ENFIELD	5 10, *5 10	10 57	8 22	10 32
to Wood Green		12 22	8 22	10 36
TOTTENHAM COURT ROAD	5 26, *4 44		8 22	10 36
to Winchmore Hill	5 26, 5 36			
to Wood Green				

First Cars from Finsbury Park to Enfield 4 56, Winchmore Hill to Finsbury
Last " Park 12 20 " from Wood Green.

35 HIGHGATE (ARCHWAY TAVERN)—ELEPHANT & CASTLE
Via Holloway Road, Upper Street, The Angel (Islington), Rosebery Avenue, Theobald's Road, Kingsway, Aldwych, Victoria Embankment and Westminster Bridge

	WEEKDAYS First Car	Last Car	SUNDAYS First Car	Last Car
From HIGHGATE (Archway Tavern)	4 39	10 4	7 35	11 30
ELEPHANT & CASTLE	5 24	10 45, 12 33	8 20	11 57
		(Sats. 3 40)		

10 56, *12 32 * From Westminster Station.
* From Westminster Station.

Another Service, 33, runs between HIGHBURY STATION and ELEPHANT & CASTLE
on Weekdays only.

37 MANOR HOUSE (FINSBURY PARK)—ALDERSGATE
Via Green Lanes, Mildmay Park, Essex Rd., The Angel (Islington) and Goswell Rd.

	First Car	Last Car
From MANOR HOUSE	5 50	7 3 Sats. 3 13
ALDERSGATE	7 16	7 33 " 3 40

Weekday Rush hours only.

41 MANOR HOUSE (FINSBURY PARK)—MOORGATE
Via Green Lanes, Mildmay Park, Southgate Road, Baring Street, East Road and City Road

	WEEKDAYS First Car	Last Car	SUNDAYS First Car	Last Car
From MANOR HOUSE	4 54	12 7 Sats. 12 0	6 28	11 34
MOORGATE	5 27	12 31 " 12 30	6 51	12 0

43 STAMFORD HILL—HOLBORN
Via Stoke Newington High Street and High Street, Kingsland High Street and Gray's Inn Road

	WEEKDAYS First Car	Last Car	SUNDAYS First Car	Last Car
From STAMFORD HILL	4 12	12 9	8 10	12 15
HOLBORN	4 48	12 43	8 42	12 50

45 STAMFORD HILL—MOORGATE
Via Stoke Newington High Street and Kingsland High Street and Road, Shoreditch Church, Old Street and City Road

	First Car	Last p.m.
From STAMFORD HILL	5 16	7 35 Sats. 2 36
MOORGATE	5 42	8 4 " 3 6

Weekdays only.

47 STAMFORD HILL—LONDON DOCKS

Via Stoke Newington High Street and Road, Kingsland High Street and Road, Shoreditch, Commercial Street, Leman Street and Dock Street

	WEEKDAYS		SUNDAYS	
From	First Car	Last Car	First Car	Last Car
STAMFORD HILL	...		9 12	
LONDON DOCKS	5 47	12 16	9 12	12 18

49 EDMONTON (TOWN HALL)—LIVERPOOL STREET STATION

Via Tottenham High Road, Stamford Hill, Stoke Newington High Street and Road, Kingsland High Street and Road and Shoreditch High Street

	WEEKDAYS		SUNDAYS	
From	First Car	Last Car	First Car	Last Car
EDMONTON (Town Hall)	5 1	11 30	7 40, *6 50	11 6
to Stamford Hill	5 49, *4 37	12 23	7 16, 7 20	12 3
LIVERPOOL STREET STATION	5 49	12 4		12 4
to Stamford Hill				

*From Stamford Hill.

Weekday Rush-Hours Extended to PONDERS END (Southbury Road).
First Car from Southbury Road 6 24 from Liverpool Street Station 5 49
Last 7 33.

51 MUSWELL HILL—BLOOMSBURY

Via Hornsey, Haringey, Green Lanes, Mildmay Park, Essex Road, The Angel (Islington), Rosebery Avenue and Theobalds Road.

	WEEKDAYS		SUNDAYS	
From	First Car	Last Car	First Car	Last Car
MUSWELL HILL	6 15, *5	11 9	10 13	11 40
to Nag's Head	5 33, †4	12 7	10 49	12 9
BLOOMSBURY	5 8	11 30	10 10	11 35
to Wellington				

*From Stamford Hill.

53 TOTTENHAM COURT ROAD—ALDGATE

Via Hampstead Road, Camden Road, Parkhurst Road, Seven Sisters Road, Finsbury Park, Camden Common, Upper Clapton Road, Lower Clapton Road, Mare Street, Cambridge Road, Whitechapel Road and High Street

	WEEKDAYS		SUNDAYS	
From	First Car	Last Car	First Car	Last Car
ALDGATE	5 44, *5	10 52	8 7	10 56
to Nag's Head	5 31	11 30	9 1, 8 7	10 16
TOTTENHAM COURT ROAD	6 57	11 30	8 3	11 35
to Stamford Hill				

*From Stamford Hill.

55 LEYTON (BAKER'S ARMS)—BLOOMSBURY

Via Lea Bridge Road, Lower Clapton Road, Mare Street, Hackney Road and Theobalds Road.

	WEEKDAYS		SUNDAYS	
From	First Car	Last Car	First Car	Last Car
LEYTON (Baker's Arms)	*5 5	11 35	*9 20	11 41
to Kenninghall Road			(To Hackney Stn. 12 3)	
BLOOMSBURY	4 57	10 46	8 54	11 7
to Kenninghall Road 3 30			8 35	
*From Kenninghall Road 3 45			*From Kenninghall 8 6	
			From Hackney 8 7	

57 LEYTON (BAKER'S ARMS)—LIVERPOOL STREET STATION

Via Lea Bridge Road, Lower Clapton Road, Mare Street, Hackney Road and Shoreditch High Street.

	WEEKDAYS		SUNDAYS	
From	First Car	Last Car	First Car	Last Car
LEYTON (Baker's Arms)	5 21	11 38	7 28	11 41
to Hackney	(to Hackney 12 48)			
LIVERPOOL STREET STATION	(5 57 from Hackney)		8 4	12 16

Sundays—First from Kenninghall Rd. to Liverpool St. 7 14. Liverpool St. to Kenninghall Road 7 43. Hackney Stn. to Baker's Arms 7 58.

59 EDMONTON (TOWN HALL)—HOLBORN

Via Tottenham High Road, Seven Sisters Road, Caledonian Road, King's Cross and Gray's Inn Road.

	WEEKDAYS		SUNDAYS	
From	First Car	Last Car	First Car	Last Car
EDMONTON (Town Hall)	4 55, *4 19	11 57, 12 32	8 57, *9 30	11 29
HOLBORN	5 23	12 23, †1 0	9 30	12 0

*From Tramway Avenue. †From Finsbury Park.

---

61 LEYTON (BAKER'S ARMS)—ALDGATE

Via Whipp's Cross Road, Leytonstone High Road, Stratford High Street and Road, Bow Road, Mile End Road and High Street

	WEEKDAYS		SUNDAYS	
From	First Car	Last Car	First Car	Last Car
BAKER'S ARMS	4 36	11 39 Sats. 11 57	8 15, *6 45	11 39
to Bow	5 4	11 58	7 6	11 58
ALDGATE	5 13	32, 4, 34, 4 53, 12 30		11 59

*From Bow 3 32, 4 13, 4 53 †From Bow 5 13 *From Bow

63 ILFORD BROADWAY—ALDGATE

Via Manor Park Broadway, Romford Road, Stratford High Street and Road, Bow Road, Mile End Road and Whitechapel Road and High Street

	WEEKDAYS		SUNDAYS	
From	First Car	Last Car	First Car	Last Car
ILFORD BROADWAY	5 1	11 33	9 3	10 48
ALDGATE	5 21	12 10	8 24	12 14

*From Stratford

65 GREEN STREET, BARKING ROAD—BLOOMSBURY

Via Barking Road, East India Dock Road, Commercial Road East, Old Street, Clerkenwell Road and Theobalds Road

	WEEKDAYS		SUNDAYS	
From	First Car	Last Car	First Car	Last Car
GREEN STREET	*6 52	7 40	7 49	
BLOOMSBURY to Iron Bridge	6 8	7 35	7 45	
CANNING TOWN to Blackwall Tunnel				
BLOOMSBURY	9 0, 1 1, 11 21, 11 32			

*From Iron Bridge 6 26 *From Blackwall Tun.
NON-RUSH HOURS between Blackwall Tunnel and Bloomsbury only.
SUNDAYS between Canning Town and Bloomsbury only.

67 BARKING BROADWAY—ALDGATE

Via Barking Road, East India Dock Road and Commercial Road East

	WEEKDAYS		SUNDAYS	
From	First Car	Last Car	First Car	Last Car
BARKING BROADWAY	5 12	11 18	8 26, 17 5	11 18
to Green Street	5 12, 4 34	11 24	from Green St.	
to Blackwall Tunnel	4 56	11 54	7 30	
ALDGATE	5 0	11 34		12 30

*From Canning Tunnel †From Canning Town

69 NORTH FINCHLEY (TALLY HO CORNER)—TOTTENHAM COURT ROAD

Via Great North Road, Archway Road, Junction Road, Kentish Town, Camden Town, High Street and Hampstead Road

NON-RUSH HOURS between Highgate (Archway Tavern) and Tottenham C.Rd. only

	WEEKDAYS		SUNDAYS	
From	First Car	Last Car	First Car	Last Car
TALLY HO CORNER	5 24	7 49	7 5	
TOTTENHAM COURT ROAD	7 36	7 5		

SUNDAYS between Wood Green and Aldgate only.

71 ALDERSGATE—WOOD GREEN—ALDGATE

Via Goswell Road, The Angel (Islington), Holloway Road, Seven Sisters Road, Finsbury Park, Harringay, Wood Green, Lordship Lane, Bruce Grove, Tottenham High Road, Clapton Common, Upper Clapton Road, Lower Clapton Road, Mare Street, Cambridge Road and High Street

	WEEKDAYS		SUNDAYS	
From	First Car	Last Car	First Car	Last Car
ALDERSGATE to Wood Green	5 2	11 37, †1 14	8 3	11 46
WOOD GREEN to Aldersgate	5 8, 6 46	11 55	8 35	11 26
to Hackney			8 2, 8 21	12 34
ALDGATE to Wood Green	5 23	11 48		
to Stamford Hill	5 55			
Hackney				

*From Stamford Hill. †From Hackney 1 9

SUNDAYS between Wood Green and Aldgate only.

75 STAMFORD HILL—HOLBORN

Via Stoke Newington High Street and Road, Balls Pond Road, Essex Road, The Angel (Islington) and Rosebery Avenue

	WEEKDAYS		SUNDAYS	
From	First Car	Last Car	First Car	Last Car
STAMFORD HILL	5 12	11 29		
HOLBORN	5 42	11 16		

Weekdays only.

77 WEST INDIA DOCKS—ALDERSGATE

Via Burdett Road, Victoria Park, Wick Road, Hackney Station, Graham Road, Balls Pond Road, Essex Road, The Angel (Islington) and Goswell Road

	WEEKDAYS		SUNDAYS	
From	First Car	Last Car	First Car	Last Car
WEST INDIA DOCKS	5 56, *5 30	10 29	11 2	
ALDERSGATE to Hackney Station	5 2	11 16	9 3, 8 9 26	11 16

*From Hackney Station.

To Burdett Rd. Poplar 11 49
from Aldersgate and Goswell Road
*Hackney Stn. 11 32

Left Panel

79
WALTHAM CROSS—SMITHFIELD MARKET
Via Edmonton, Tottenham High Road, Seven Sisters Road, Holloway Road, Upper Street, The Angel (Islington) and St. John Street.

From	WEEKDAYS		SUNDAYS	
	First Car	Last Car	First Car	Last Car
WALTHAM CROSS	4 45	10 14	9 5 7 55	10 16
to Finsbury Park	4 54	12 3	9 5 5	12 3
to Tramway Avenue	4 54	12 3		
SMITHFIELD MARKET	5 50	11 10	9 40	11 37
to Tramway Avenue				

First Tramway Avenue to Waltham Cross 4 34
* From Finsbury Park 12 39
First Edmonton to Waltham Cross 3 39

81
EPPING FOREST (RISING SUN)—BLOOMSBURY
Via Whipps Cross, Lea Bridge Road, Clapton Road, Graham Road, Balls Pond Road, Essex Road, Angel (Islington) and Rosebery Avenue.

From	WEEKDAYS		SUNDAYS	
	First Car	Last Car	First Car	Last Car
RISING SUN	5 55	8	9 54	10 56
BLOOMSBURY	6 24	11 0	9 29	11 26
to Whipps Cross	6 24	12 5	8 29	12 5
to Baker's Arms	6 24	12 18	8 25	12 43
to Kenninghall Road				
to Hackney Station	5 37		8 9	

Hackney Station to Whipps Cross 7 15, Baker's Arms 5 56, Hackney Station 5 58
* From Whipps Cross 7 15, Baker's Arms 11 4, Hackney Station 5 58

83
STAMFORD HILL—MOORGATE
Via Stoke Newington High Street and Road, Balls Pond Road, Southgate Road, Baring Street, East Road and City Road. *Weekdays only.*

From	First Car	Last Car
STAMFORD HILL	6 49	8 8
MOORGATE	7 19	8 24

LEYTON AND WEST HAM SERVICES 7 & 8.

7
LEYTON (BAKER'S ARMS)—DOCKS. Via Leyton High Road, Stratford Broadway and Freemasons Road.

From	WEEKDAYS		SUNDAYS	
	First Car	Last Car	First Car	Last Car
BAKER'S ARMS	5 24, 5 0	9 15	9 0	11 7
to Stratford		11 20		11 30
DOCKS	5 18, 5 1	10 25, *11 48	9 0, *9 37	10 55
to Stratford		10 55		

8
LEYTON (BAKER'S ARMS)—DOCKS. Via Leyton High Road, Cann Hall Road, Upton Lane, Plaistow Broadway, Balaam Street and Freemasons Road.

From	WEEKDAYS		SUNDAYS	
	First Car	Last Car	First Car	Last Car
BAKER'S ARMS	4 46	9 54	9 0	11 27
to Wanstead Flats		10 35	8 34	11 28
DOCKS	5 42	10 50, *11 31	9 30, *9 24	10 45, *11 28

* From Wanstead Flats.

SOUTHERN SECTION

NOTE.—Services running the whole length of Victoria Embankment are numbered:—

}	2	16	22
}	4	18	24
	36	66	84
	38	56	72
			76
			80

2
WIMBLEDON HILL—VICTORIA EMBANKMENT.
Via Merton, Tooting Broadway, Balham, Clapham Road, Kennington.

From	WEEKDAYS		SUNDAYS	
	First Car	Last Car	First Car	Last Car
WIMBLEDON HILL	5 44	11 37, *12 21	9 3, *7 55	11 56, *12 23
EMBANKMENT, Savoy Street	4 45	10 57	8 30	11 51
to Clapham	4 45	12 0	8 25	11 59, *1 1
to Merton	4 45	12 18	8 25	12 0

First Embankment from Tooting B'way 4 31 from Merton 5 40
* from Clapham to Merton 12 0, to Wimbledon 4 21

Service 4a runs between Merton and Victoria Embankment in Weekday rush hours only.

* From Clapham. † From Merton.

Right Panel

4
WIMBLEDON HILL—VICTORIA EMBANKMENT
Via Merton, Tooting Broadway, Balham, Clapham Road, Kennington.

From	WEEKDAYS		SUNDAYS	
	First Car	Last Car	First Car	Last Car
WIMBLEDON HILL	*4 52, 5 24	11 37, *12 21	7 46, *9 15	11 56, *12 23
EMBANKMENT, Savoy Street	5 11	10 58	8 22	11 55
to Tooting	5 11	12 0	8 31	12 0
to Clapham	5 11	12 5	5 43, 8 32	12 25
to Wimbledon			5 11	12 25

First from Clapham to Merton 3 34
to Wimbledon 4 21
* to Wimbledon 7 21, 8 29
to Merton to Wimbledon B'wy 7 14
to Tooting B'wy 5 12
to Blackfriars 5 29

Service 4a runs between Merton and Victoria Embankment in Weekday rush hours.

* From Merton. † From The Plough, Clapham.

6
SOUTHCROFT ROAD (Junction with Mitcham Lane)—**SOUTHWARK BRIDGE**
Via Southcroft Road, Tooting Broadway, Balham, Clapham Road, Kennington Park Road, Elephant and Castle and St. George's Church.

From	WEEKDAYS		SUNDAYS	
	First Car	Last Car	First Car	Last Car
SOUTHCROFT ROAD	5 53	8 11	9 6	11 38
to St. George's Church		12 15	9 1	11 52
to "Plough," Clapham			7 1	11 19
SOUTHWARK BRIDGE	7 1	8 58, †11 32	8 56	
		(to Plough 12 41)	to Plough 11 25	

SATS. p.m. & SUNS. Southcroft Rd. and St. Geo.'s Ch. only.
SUNDAYS
49 8, †8 2 Last Car
8 56 to Plough 11 39

ST. GEORGE'S CHURCH *Sats.*, (to Plough 12 41)
* From St. George's Church. † From Plough, Clapham.

8
TOOTING JUNCTION—VICTORIA STATION
Via Tooting Broadway, Balham, Clapham Road, South Lambeth Road, Vauxhall Bridge.

From	WEEKDAYS		SUNDAYS	
	First Car	Last Car	First Car	Last Car
TOOTING JUNCTION	5 13	10 55	8 13	11 43
to "The Plough"	5 13, 5 54	11 16		11 35
VICTORIA STATION to "The Plough"	5 53	11 26	7 36	11 19
		to B'way 12 41		

* From Plough, Clapham.

10
TOOTING BROADWAY—SOUTHWARK BRIDGE
Via Southcroft Road, Mitcham Lane, Streatham, Brixton, Kennington Park Road, St. George's Church.

From	WEEKDAYS		SUNDAYS	
	First Car	Last Car	First Car	Last Car
TOOTING BROADWAY	5 0, 6 10, *5 1	8 6	8 16, *7 22	11 45
to St. George's Church	5 0, 6 10, 14	12 5	7 32, †6 38	12 0
to Streatham	5 55, 5 0, 6 50	12 9		
SOUTHWARK Bridge	*4 40, †4 46	11 28		
TOOTING BROADWAY		11 44		

Sats., (to Streatham 12 34)
ST. GEORGE'S CHURCH to Streatham 12 40
* From St. George's Church. † From Streatham. † From Telford Avenue.

Sats. p.m. & Suns. Tooting Broadway & St. Geo.'s Ch. only.

12
TOOTING JUNCTION—HOP EXCHANGE (NEAR LONDON BRIDGE)
Via Tooting Broadway, Garrat Lane, York Road, Battersea Park Road, Vauxhall Station, Lambeth Road, Borough Road and Southwark Bridge Road.

From	WEEKDAYS		SUNDAYS	
	First Car	Last Car	First Car	Last Car
TOOTING JUNCTION	*4 46	10 16	9 0	10 41
to Princes Vauxhall	4 48	12 21	9 0	11 22
to Jew's Row	4 48	12 22	9 0	12 1
HOP EXCHANGE	5 18	11 11	7 55, 8 54	11 40
Vauxhall to Wandsworth High St.			7 55, 8 54	11 1
Princes Head			† Wandsworth 7 11, 8 10	12 11
			Earlsfield to Vauxh 16 21	

* From Prince's Head 4 41

14
EARLSFIELD STATION—HOP EXCHANGE (NEAR LONDON BRIDGE)
Via York Road, Battersea Park Road, Vauxhall Station, Westminster Bridge, Victoria Embankment, Blackfriars Bridge and Southwark Street.

From	First Car	Last Car
EARLSFIELD STATION	4 47	9 7
HOP EXCHANGE	6 47	8 9
Blackfriars to Barnfield	8 8	9 3
to High St., Wandsworth	4 53	11 30

Week Days only.
NON-RUSH HOURS between High St., Wandsworth and Hop Exchange only.

32 From LAVENDER HILL to Queen's Road, CHELSEA BRIDGE to Queen's Road — LAVENDER HILL—CHELSEA BRIDGE Via Queen's Road, Battersea

34 KING'S ROAD, CHELSEA—SOUTHWARK BRIDGE
Via Beaufort Street, Battersea Bridge, Battersea Park Road, Falcon Road, Clapham Junction, Queen's Road, Lavender Hill, Wandsworth Road, Stockwell Road, Brixton, Coldharbour Lane, Camberwell Green, Walworth Road, Elephant & Castle and St. George's Church.

From KING'S ROAD
" to Camberwell Green.
" to The Plough.
SOUTHWARK BRIDGE
" to Clapham Junction.
Clapham Junction to King's Road
The Plough " "
Camberwell Gn. to King's Road
" to Southwark
" to King's Road

36 ABBEY WOOD—VICTORIA EMBANKMENT
Via Beresford Square (Woolwich), Greenwich Church, Greenwich Road, New Cross Road,
Old Kent Road and Elephant & Castle.
From ABBEY WOOD to New Cross Gate.
" to New Cross.
EMBANKMENT to Beresford Square
" to New Cross.
" to Blackwall Lane

38 ABBEY WOOD—VICTORIA EMBANKMENT
Via Beresford Square (Woolwich), Greenwich Church, Greenwich Road, New Cross,
Old Kent Road and Elephant & Castle.
From ABBEY WOOD to New Cross Gate.
EMBANKMENT, Savoy Street

40 ABBEY WOOD—SAVOY STREET, STRAND Via Beresford Square (Woolwich),
Greenwich Church, Greenwich Rd., New Cross Rd., Peckham Rd., Camberwell Green,
Kennington Rd. and WESTMINSTER BRIDGE
From ABBEY WOOD to New Cross Gate.
" to King's Cross
SAVOY' STREET to King's Wm. St.

46 BERESFORD SQUARE, WOOLWICH—SOUTHWARK BRIDGE Via Academy Road, Well
Hall Road, Eltham, Lee Green, Lewisham High Road, New Cross Road, Old Kent Road,
Great Dover Street and St. George's Church.
From BERESFORD SQUARE
SOUTHWARK BRIDGE to New Cross
" to Eltham
" to Lee Green

---

16 NORBURY—VICTORIA EMBANKMENT Via Streatham, Brixton, Kennington
From NORBURY to Telford Av.
EMBANKMENT, Savoy Street

18 NORBURY—VICTORIA EMBANKMENT Via Streatham, Brixton, Kennington
From NORBURY, Savoy Street
EMBANKMENT, Savoy Street
" to Telford Avenue

20 SOUTHCROFT ROAD (Junction with Mitcham Lane)—VICTORIA STATION
Via Mitcham Lane, Streatham, Brixton, Vauxhall Bridge
From SOUTHCROFT ROAD to Telford Av.
VICTORIA " to Southcroft Road

22 SOUTHCROFT ROAD (Mitcham Lane)—VICTORIA EMBANKMENT
Via Mitcham Lane, Streatham, Brixton, Kennington
SOUTHCROFT ROAD, Savoy Street
EMBANKMENT, Savoy Street

24 SOUTHCROFT ROAD (Mitcham Lane)—VICTORIA EMBANKMENT
Via Mitcham Lane, Streatham, Brixton, Kennington
SOUTHCROFT ROAD, Savoy Street
EMBANKMENT, Savoy Street

26 KEW BRIDGE—HOP EXCHANGE (NEAR LONDON BRIDGE)
Via Chiswick High Road, Hammersmith Broadway, Putney Bridge, High Street
(Wandsworth), Clapham Junction, Wandsworth Road, Vauxhall Station, Albert Embank-
ment, Westminster Bridge, Victoria Embankment
From KEW BRIDGE
" to Putney
" to Hammersmith Broadway
HOP EXCHANGE
" to Chiswick Depot
Young's Corner to York Road
York Road to Kew Bridge

28 HARROW ROAD, NEAR WILLESDEN JUNCTION—VICTORIA STATION
Via Scrubs Lane, Wood Lane, Shepherds Bush, Hammersmith Broadway, Putney
Bridge, High Street (Wandsworth), Clapham Junction
From HARROW ROAD
" to York Road
" to York Road
" to Hammersmith
VICTORIA " to Hammersmith Broadway

30 SUDBURY—TOOTING JUNCTION
Wembley, Stonebridge Park, Harlesden (Jubilee Clock), Willesden, Scrubs Lane, Wood Lane,
Shepherds Bush, Hammersmith Broadway, Putney Bridge, High St. (Wandsworth),
Garratt Lane and Tooting Broadway
From SUDBURY to York Road
" to Hammersmith
TOOTING JUNCTION to Hammersmith

50 BLACKWALL TUNNEL—FOREST HILL
Via South Street, Lewisham Road, Catford, and Stanstead Road

From	First Car	Last Car	
BLACKWALL TUNNEL ...	6 39, *6 9	7 4	*Weekday rush hours only,*
" to Catford ...	6 39, *6 9	8 24	
FOREST HILL	6 39	7 42	

*From Greenwich Church.

52 SOUTHEND VILLAGE—SOUTHWARK BRIDGE
Via Catford, Lewisham High Road, New Cross Road, Old Kent Road, Great Dover Street and St. George's Church

From	First Car	Last Car	
SOUTHEND VILLAGE ...	6 31, *4 0, *6 3	6 10 *Sats.* 3 9	*Weekday rush hours only.*
SOUTHWARK BRIDGE ...	6 45	7 0 " 3 56	
" to Catford ...	5 25	7 0	
" to New Cross	4 43	7 0	
First from New Cross Gate to Southwark Bridge	4 20, 5 5		
" " Catford ...	3 40, 5 44		
" " Southend Village	6 5		* From Catford.

54 SOUTHEND VILLAGE—VICTORIA STATION
Via Catford, Lewisham, New Cross Road, Peckham Road, Camberwell Green, Kennington and Vauxhall Bridge

From	WEEKDAYS First Car	WEEKDAYS Last Car	SUNDAYS First Car	SUNDAYS Last Car
SOUTHEND VILLAGE ...	*5 2, 5 52	11 13	*8 38	11 22
" to New Cross	*5 2, 5 52	12 23	*8 38	12 26
VICTORIA STATION ...	5 24	11 29	7 49	11 29
" " to Catford ...	+5 24	11 38	+7 1	11 31
" " to New Cross	+5 24	12 8	6 22	12 20

First, New Cross to Southend Village 4 36
*From Catford 5 0, from New Cross 4 51
† " Camberwell Green 4 26
*From Catford 5.32, 6.19, 7.15
† " New Cross 5.9, 6.3
Last Catf'd to C'well 11.39

56 PECKHAM RYE—VICTORIA EMBANKMENT
Via East Dulwich Road, Dog Kennel Hill, Denmark Hill, Camberwell Green, Walworth Road and Elephant & Castle

From	WEEKDAYS First Car	WEEKDAYS Last Car	SUNDAYS First Car	SUNDAYS Last Car
PECKHAM RYE	5 4, *5 3	11 44, *12 13	9 3, *8 34	11 31
" to Camb. Green	5 4	12 21	9 3	12 18
EMBANKMENT, Savoy Street	5 43, *4 45	11 1	8 56, *8 48	11 38
" " to Camb. Green	5 43	11 31	8 56	12 10

*From Camberwell Green

58 CATFORD—VICTORIA STATION
Via Forest Hill, Lordship Lane, Dog Kennel Hill, Denmark Hill, Camberwell Green, Kennington and Vauxhall Bridge

SUNDAYS *Extended to* BLACKWALL TUNNEL

From	WEEKDAYS First Car	WEEKDAYS Last Car	SUNDAYS First Car	SUNDAYS Last Car
CATFORD	5 18	11 13		
" to Camberwell Green ...	5 18	11 44		
VICTORIA STATION	5 3	10 54		
" " to Forest Hill ...	5 3	11 34		
" " to Dulwich Lib'y	5 3	11 56		
" " to Camb. Green	5 3	12 5		
BLACKWALL TUNNEL ...	—	—	8 46	11 2
" to Camb. Green	—	—	8 46	11 50
VICTORIA STATION ...	—	—	7 31	10 44
" " to Gr'nwich Ch.	—	—	7 17	11 24
" " to Catford ...	—	—	6 59	11 24
" " Forest Hill ...	—	—	6 59	12 2
" " to Camb. Green	—	—	6 14	12 20

First to Victoria from Forest Hill 5 5, Camberwell Green 4 37
First to Catford from Camb. Green, 4 43, to Forest Hill 4 39
Last to Camberwell Green from Forest Hill ... 12 15
from Dulwich Library ... 12 29
from Goose Green ... 12 46

First from Victoria to Goose Green ... 6 14
From Camb. Green to Goose Grn. ... 5 34
to Catford ... 6 14
From Gr'nwch to Vict. 7 55
" Catford to Vict. 6 45
" Goose Gn. to Vict. 5 45

60 DULWICH LIBRARY—SOUTHWARK BRIDGE
Via Dog Kennel Hill, Denmark Hill, Camberwell Green, Walworth Road and Elephant & Castle

From	First Car	Last Car	
DULWICH LIBRARY ...	6 40, *5 32	6 57, *Sats.* 1 47	*Weekday rush hours only.*
SOUTHWARK BRIDGE ...	6 2	7 3, *Sats.* 2 24	*From C'well Green.

62 BLACKWALL TUNNEL—SAVOY STREET, STRAND
Via South Street, Lewisham Road, Catford, Forest Hill, Lordship Lane, Dog Kennel Hill, Denmark Hill, Camberwell Green, Walworth Road, Elephant & Castle and WESTMINSTER BRIDGE—*Weekdays only.*

From	First Car	Last Car
BLACKWALL TUNNEL	5 55	10 19
" " to Camb. Green ...	5 55	11 12
" " to Forest Hill ...	5 34	11 12, 11 45 from Blackwall Lane
Greenwich Church to " "	5 22	
SAVOY STREET	7 23	9 45

First to Tunnel from Camberwell Green 6 10, from Forest Hill 4 51.
Last from Savoy Street to Blackwall Lane 10.25, Greenwich Church 10.33, Lewisham Obelisk 10.57, Forest Hill 11.37, Dulwich Library 11.45. Last from Forest Hill to Lewisham Obelisk 12 19, to Camberwell Green 12 25

66 FOREST HILL—VICTORIA EMBANKMENT
Via Brockley Rise and Road, New Cross, Peckham Road, Camberwell Green, Walworth Road, and Elephant and Castle

From	WEEKDAYS First Car	WEEKDAYS Last Car	SUNDAYS First Car	SUNDAYS Last Car
FOREST HILL	5 8	11 31	8 41, *7 44	11 35
" to Blackfriars ...	*4 47	To New X 12 39		To New X 12 32
EMBANKMENT, Savoy Street ...	6 4	11 34	8 15	11 26
" to New Cross ...	6 4	12 28	8 15	12 30
New Cross to Forest Hill ...	3 46, 4 24		8 21	

* From Cranston Road 4 3, New Cross 4 11
* From New Cross.

68 GREENWICH CHURCH—WATERLOO STATION
Via Bridge Street, Creek Road, Evelyn Street, Lower Road, Union Road, Jamaica Road, Parkers Row, Dock Head, Tooley Street, Tower Bridge Road, New Kent Road and Elephant & Castle

From	WEEKDAYS First Car	WEEKDAYS Last Car	SUNDAYS First Car	SUNDAYS Last Car
GREENWICH CHURCH	6 17	10 55	9 4	10 50
WATERLOO STATION	6 52	11 33	9 6	11 28

First from
Greenwich Church to Elephant & Castle ... 4 49
Tower Bridge to Waterloo Station 6 36
Elephant & Castle to Greenwich Church ... 5 11

First Tower Bge to Waterloo 8 53
Last Greenwich to Tower Bge 11 22

70 GREENWICH CHURCH—LONDON BRIDGE (TOOLEY ST.)
Via Bridge Street, Creek Road, Evelyn Street, Lower Road, Union Road, Jamaica Road, Parkers Row, Dock Head and Tooley Street.

From	WEEKDAYS First Car	WEEKDAYS Last Car	SUNDAYS First Car	SUNDAYS Last Car
GREENWICH CHURCH ...	4 20	11 30	7 46	11 19
" to Tower Bridge ...	4 20	12 16	7 46	11 46
LONDON BRIDGE	4 55, *4 14	12 0	7 20	11 50

* From Elephant & Castle.

72 FOREST HILL—VICTORIA EMBANKMENT
Via Brockley Rise and Road, New Cross, Peckham Road, Camberwell Green, Walworth Road and Elephant & Castle

From	WEEKDAYS First Car	WEEKDAYS Last Car	SUNDAYS First Car	SUNDAYS Last Car
FOREST HILL	6 34	11 37	8 59, *7 32	11 39
			To New X	12 32
EMBANKMENT, Savoy Street ...	†6 49	11 40	8 3	11 38
" to New Cross ...	†6 49	12 34	8 3	12 33
New Cross to Forest Hill ...	3 46, 4 24		8 21	

† From Blackfriars 4 44
* From New Cross.

74 FOREST HILL—BLACKFRIARS.
Via Brockley Rise and Road, New Cross Road, Old Kent Road, Elephant and Blackfriars Bridge

From	First Car	Last Car	
FOREST HILL	6 42	6 5 *Sats.* 1 18 p.m.	*Weekday*
BLACKFRIARS	7 31	6 57 " 2 10 "	*Rush hours only.*

76 NORWOOD—VICTORIA EMBANKMENT
Via Herne Hill Station, Brixton, Kennington Road & WESTMINSTER BRIDGE

From	WEEKDAYS First Car	WEEKDAYS Last Car	SUNDAYS First Car	SUNDAYS Last Car
NORWOOD	5 7	11 12 *Sats.* 10 55	2 53 p.m.	10 25
EMBANKMENT, Savoy Street	5 42	12 1	3 29 p.m.	11 0

78 NORWOOD—VICTORIA STATION
Via Herne Hill Station, Brixton, Stockwell Road, South Lambeth Road and Vauxhall Bridge

From	WEEKDAYS First Car	WEEKDAYS Last Car	SUNDAYS First Car	SUNDAYS Last Car
NORWOOD	5 27	11 28	8 12	11 34
VICTORIA STATION	6 0	12 6	8 45	12 8

80 NORWOOD—VICTORIA EMBANKMENT
Via Herne Hill Station, Coldharbour Lane, Camberwell Green, Walworth Road, Elephant and BLACKFRIARS BRIDGE

From	WEEKDAYS First Car	WEEKDAYS Last Car	SUNDAYS First Car	SUNDAYS Last Car
NORWOOD	5 1	11 20 *Sats.* 11 23	8 34	10 18
to Camberwell Green ...	5 1	11 56 " 11 55	8 34	11 40
EMBANKMENT, Savoy Street ...	5 44	*11 49 " *11 32	9 14	*11 1

* From Camberwell Green 12 17
*From Camb'll Gn. 12 0
Sunday cars, until the afternoon, are between Norwood and Blackfriars only.

82 HARROW ROAD, NEAR WILLESDEN JUNCTION—TOOTING JUNCTION
Via Scrubs Lane, Wood Lane, Shepherd's Bush, Hammersmith Broadway, Putney Bridge, High St. (Wandsworth), Garratt Lane & Tooting Bdway.

From	WEEKDAYS First Car	WEEKDAYS Last Car	SUNDAYS First Car	SUNDAYS Last Car
HARROW ROAD ...	5 26, *4 22	10 42	7 32, 8 24, 9 32	10 31
" to York Road	5 26, *4 22	11 52	7 32, 8 24, 9 32	11 37
" to Hammersmith	5 26	12 20	7 32, 8 24, 9 32	12 28
TOOTING JUNCTION ...	+5 6	11 21	8 30, 9 24 *7 13	11 29
York Road to Hammersmith	5 12	12 30	—	12 16

+From Hammersmith 5 6, Putney Bge. 5 10, York Road 5 12
·* From Hammersmith

84 PECKHAM RYE—VICTORIA EMBANKMENT
Via East Dulwich Road, Dog Kennel Hill, Denmark Hill, Camberwell Green, Walworth Road, and Elephant & Castle

From	First Car	Last Car	
PECKHAM RYE	6 10, *5 27	10 57, *11 14	*Weekdays only.*
EMBANKMENT, Savoy Street	5 26, *4 45	11 41	* From Camberwell Green.
" to Camberwell Green	5 26	12 5	

This trailer car No. T116 was one of a batch of 150 built by Brush in 1915. The combination seen in the photograph is on the circular Victoria Embankment– Norbury service on which the trailer cars were only used. They all were withdrawn by 1924.   *O.J. Morris*

This commercial postcard (posted in 1909) shows the 'E1' class tramcar No. 800 built in 1907 by Hurst Nelson. A single deck 'G' class car is seen in the distance of Upper Street, Islington North.   *Author's Collection*

With the number of electric cars building rapidly to over a thousand, a number of depots were required, some of which could be taken over from the horse-trams, though very different facilities were needed, especially inspection-pits. To save space, all were designed to be filled by traversers, which could pack in more cars in less space than pointwork could. Depots were set up at Abbey Wood, Bow, Brixton Hill, Camberwell, Clapham, Hackney, Hammersmith, Hampstead, Stamford Hill, Leyton, Holloway, New Cross, Norwood, Poplar, Streatham and Wandsworth. The need for a central repair depot soon became urgent, and it was decided to site this in Charlton, on vacant industrial land on the east side of the South Eastern & Chatham Railway's branch from Blackheath Tunnel to Angerstein's Wharf on the Thames; this would enable heavy equipment to be received on rail wagons into the Works. Work began on the project in 1906, several years before the tramtracks arrived at its front door; when they did, a short branch was laid into the Works, off the Woolwich Road line just east of the railway bridge, the junction facing towards London.

The depot was finally ready in 1909 and handled all repair and rebuilding work for lines south of the Thames. In 1926 it was extended to enable cars from north of the river to be handled. The layout comprised first a short siding to the right which ran into the stores department and was usually filled with staff cars and repainted cars ready to leave. It then went through the main gate and the conduit ran off left and terminated; movement from then on was by steam shunting engine. This was an 0–4–0ST by Andrew Barclay (No. 991 of 1904) purchased in 1908. Ahead was the connection to the railway, the embankment of which lay on the left hand side, and to the right the main buildings, the smithy, foundry and machine shop on the left (west) side, a traverser in the centre and a body shop on the east side. Above were departments dealing in such things as roller blinds. Some fitting was still done at other depots and a common sight at Charlton was one of the small open wheel-cars setting off for a depot with renewed wheel-sets.

The LCC was also able to make use of other facilities it had; there was a wharf on Deptford Creek for handling setts, cement etc. Battersea wharf, which was alongside Battersea bridge and adjacent to the tramway across the river to Kings Road, was where sand was imported; this had to be distributed to depots every day. Cars were supposed to leave their depots with full hoppers, but on a wet day it was soon exhausted, and supplies for topping up were kept at change-points. The Tramway did not rely only on its service trams; it had a fleet of steam and later motor service lorries, some equipped with cranes. Because these vehicles did very little mileage they lasted long; in the late 1920s the LCCT were still running a number of British Berna lorries, a Swiss marque which had long gone, and Ensigns; the Foden steam lorries also lasted well.

Although there was a lot of competition between trams and buses, there was none between different tramway operators, owing to the adoption of separate areas. Indeed there was always co-operation. For example on the Kilburn Lane to Kensal Green line the County boundary ran down the middle of the street, so that the LCC owned the westbound and MET the eastbound track, but for most of the time the MET worked both. Route 89

This 1908 scene near the Elephant and Castle shows the tram 'dominant', with a 'Great Eastern' motor bus running through to Leyton, which the tram (at that time) could not do. Note the Hansom cab on the left of the picture and a 'growler' cab on the right.

Tramway and Railway World

from Acton to Putney was in fact an LUT line as far as Hammersmith, and LCC beyond, but worked throughout by LCC, and in the rush hours from 1931 by both LUT and LCC cars.

The LCCT never ceased to think in terms of expansion, and as late as 1st October, 1931 opened a new double-line tramway from Well Hall Road Eltham along Westhorne Avenue, by-passing the town; owing to having to build a new railway bridge, the section from this bridge to Middle Park Avenue did not open until the following 30th June.

Turning now to the tramcars themselves, during the few years the horse-cars carried the LCC title there was no change except in the case of the Brixton Hill service, already mentioned. Electrification however brought more radical change than might have been the case, for the first cars to be purchased were bogie cars, almost doubling the size of those they replaced. Some other systems, which switched from horse-cars to four-wheeled electric trams, saw a less dramatic change. The dithering by the Council did have one advantage; between 1898 when the matter was first broached, and 1903 when the first cars arrived, there had been a rapid evolution of car design, so that the LCC's first type, the 'A' type, seemed a good deal more modern than the first LUT cars delivered two years earlier.

The Dick, Kerr bodies seated 66; the lower saloon had two large windows and four small each side; seating was longitudinal. The top deck was open and had garden seating. There was no trolley-standard, as working beyond the conduit was not thought of. The plough carrier was fitted to the inside end of one of the bogies, which had an extension for this. In common with other early LCC cars, there were three lights above the destination box, which by permutations of colour supplied an indication of route, before (in 1912) numbers were decided upon. This was a small perpetuation of the system adopted by some horse-tram operators of having cars on different routes painted different colours. This had been common with horse-buses, and indeed was adopted for a time by some motor buses.

It was realised that 66 seats were not needed on all routes, and a smaller car, the 'B' type, was ordered seating only 56, running on four wheels. The LCC ordered its cars by the hundred (the only municipal operator who could afford this luxury). The decision at this time to number the original training car of 1900 No. 101 meant that though the 'A' class were 1–100, the 'B' class was 102–201, with repercussions on the 'C', 'D' and 'E' car series. The 'B' class cars had three windows to the lower saloon, and open tops, and were similar to the cars on scores of town systems now being built up and down the country. The very similar 'C' class (202–301) came on to the streets in 1905. It was always said that drivers disliked the 'Bs' and liked the 'Cs'; but both were built on Brill 21E trucks, the only difference being that the 'B' class had DK24A motors and the 'Cs' had Westinghouse motors. Covered tops were fitted from 1906.

The next class, 'D', was a return to a bogie type; they looked the same as the 'A' class but were by different builders: Nos. 302–376 by Brush of Loughborough, and Nos. 377–401 by the British Electric Car Co. of Trafford Park, Manchester, though the equipment was common to both. The 'D' class received covered tops in 1906, first with open balconies, later totally-enclosed. This class was the first to be fitted with magnetic brakes and a few also had trolley poles quite early on.

LCCT wheel-car No. 012 (Mountain & Gibson Truck) seen here having been shunted out of the Charlton depot by the steam locomotive (*left*) in April 1930. A 'B' class staff car No. 158 is in the siding on the right. *Author*

The Charlton depot in April 1930 seen here from the main gate. The end of the conduit can be seen (*bottom left*) with no power being available after that. Two class 'E1' cars are being finished off (*left*) with beyond, the lower decks of new 'E1' class cars of the 552–601 series, just delivered on rail wagons (via the connection to the SR behind the cars). In attendance is breakdown wagon B5, an Ensign. The blacksmiths and wheel shop are housed in the smaller buildings. *Author*

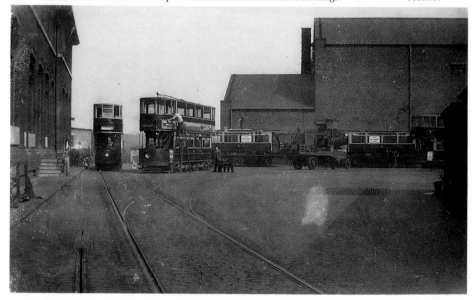

The first of the 'E' class cars appeared in 1907; together with the improved 'E1' type slightly longer and wider, there were to be 1,300 of these placed on LCC metals, and some would last to the end. There were still the long seats in the saloon, but the upper decks were more spacious, with very convenient crescent-shaped seats at the ends. Construction continued until 1922, and naturally not all were identically-equipped. 975 bodies were built by Hurst Nelson with 275 by Brush; however 50 were built by LCC itself. Trucks were by Mountain & Gibson, Hurst, Nelson and Heenan & Froude; motors were either Westinghouse 200 ('E' class) or 220 ('E1s') or Metropolitan Vickers 121 or Dick, Kerr 31c. It was a magnificent tram, very reliable, seating up to 78 persons depending on arrangement, and steady to ride in. For most people who recall the LCC trams, it is this one they remember.

Two batches of single-deck cars were built in 1906–8 for working through the Kingsway Tunnel: class 'F' Nos. 552–567, class 'G' Nos. 568–601; they were however almost identical, both seating 36 with longitudinal seats, with five windows to the saloon and a clerestory roof. These cars only worked from the Angel to a terminus in the tunnel under Aldwych until 10th April, 1908, when the Embankment line was completed, and the lower part of the tunnel; thereafter the single deck cars ran from Highbury to various points, altered over the years: Lavender Hill, Clapham, and for a short time Kennington Gate. All cars were withdrawn in 1930 when conversion of the tunnel to take double deck cars was begun; their trucks were used for a new series of 'E1' class cars (Nos. 552–601).

In 1911 the notion was propounded that single-deck cars coupled in pairs would be preferable to double-deckers – after all, this was the system used all over Europe. So trials were carried out on the Hampstead Road, but the idea was abandoned. Nevertheless the possibility of letting double-deck cars tow trailers was also mooted, and trials made in 1913 on the Eltham route, using converted horse-cars as trailers. It seemed to work, provided a circular route or one with a turning circle was used, and in July 1914 150 trailers cars (4-wheeled) were ordered from Brush. These came in very handy for the increased traffic of the War years; they were withdrawn however in 1922. The original idea had been to use the powerful new 4-wheeled tram, the 'M' class, to tow, but in fact the 'E1s' were mainly used.

The 'M' class was intended as a modern four-wheeler with enough power to cope successfully with steep gradients. It was of unusual design, having a pressed steel frame with no exterior springs; the three-window covered-top body was pivoted at the ends of the frame, where also the plough carrier (when used) was fitted. The prototype, No. 1427, was built in 1909 and the others followed from 1910. The first ten went to Abbey Wood direct by rail, erected at the depot, and had twin booms (the Royal Observatory insisted on a return wire on lines passing near it), and had no plough. Some came out with ploughs but no booms; from 1913 a number were also fitted with trailer-towing gear. The cars seated up to 62, and with the same motor power as the 'E1' this four-wheeler was a smart runner. After 1933 it was able to take over some duties from 'borough' lines whose cars, though only some six years older, were no longer fit for duty.

From 1926 a policy of 'Pullmanisation' of the 'E1' class was put in hand, upholstered seats replacing the old slat seats; at the same time a new livery of bright red and cream was applied as they went through shops; the same thing was done with the 'M' class. Other classes retained the chocolate and cream livery until withdrawn.

In 1930 the first of the 'E3' cars appeared; these were not too dissimilar from the 'E1' but did present a more modern appearance; at the same time another class, the 'HR1' (of which there was only one, No. 1852) and the 'HR2' went into service, a 'hilly route' car with eight equal wheels and four motors, but still retaining the outward appearance of the 'E1' as far as the body went. On 14th January, 1931 the enlarged Kingsway Subway was opened, at a ceremony using car No. 1931 ('E3') in white livery with blue lining; at the press show there was also an 'E1' car fitted with a windscreen; this was standard on the 'E3' class, but was not fitted to the first few 'HR2s'.

Meanwhile the former single-deck subway cars had been sent to Charlton and fitted with new 'E1' frames and bodies, only the trucks being re-used.

In 1932, and not before time, the LCC produced a tram which could hold a candle against the 'company lines' UCC cars in terms of modern styling. This was a special 'HR2' car numbered 1, put out in an eye-catching livery of blue and ivory; it was named the Bluebird. It was longer, wider, and lower and was fitted with a seat for the driver, three kinds of brake (manual, magnetic and air) and air-operated sanders.

Another experiment of the time was the fitting of an 'E1' car (No. 795) with patterned aluminium exterior panelling, unpainted. Another new 'class' was the 'ME/3', but this was simply three 'M' class cars with lengthened bodies placed on 'E1' trucks.

This poor photograph is of a class 'K' LCC tramways box van No. 09 of 1908 seen here bowling along the road near Woolwich Arsenal in April 1932.   *Author*

The first batch of 'M' class cars were constructed by Hurst Nelson; this one, No. 1438, is seen on Leyton Route 8 after having been moved from Abbey Wood depot; the place is Wanstead Flats. Some of these cars were supplied to Leyton for mileage allowance against Leyton cars using LCC tracks.

Author

A LCCT tower-wagon built on the chassis of a former Tilling-Stevens petrol-electric bus at Hammersmith in March 1932. Note the livery with the shield logo. *Author*

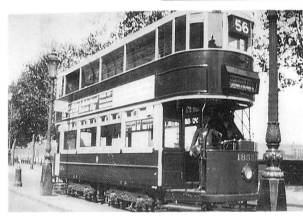

Fifty 'HR2' class cars were ordered from English Electric in 1930, to be built on EMB trucks. Here one of the first is seen on the Embankment on 7th July, No. 1855, not yet fitted with windscreens. *Author*

The Charlton Works steam locomotive, an Andrew Barclay No. 991 of 1904, purchased by the LCC from Beckton Gasworks in 1908. It has just drawn re-painted class 'E1' car No. 973 out of the works and placed it in the Stores Department spur which was outside the gates and had the electric conduit.
Author

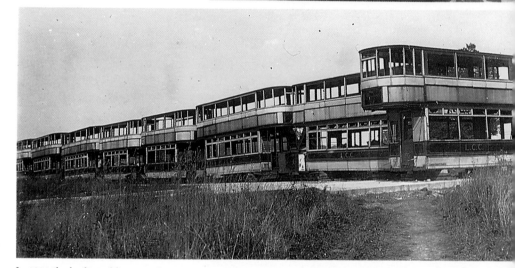

In 1931 the bodies of four 'A' class cars, three 'C' class and one 'D' class trams were dumped on a building plot at Sidcup, whether for scrapping or use as huts was not clear at the time the photograph was taken. *Author*

The track on Dog Kennel Hill, East Dulwich, was four-tracked in 1912 to minimise the chance of collisions due to cars running away. Some 'C' class had special cam-operated track brakes for this hill; the car photographed here is a class 'HR2'. *Author*

After 1933 the cars continued in their old livery for some time; the 'A', 'B', 'C', and 'D' class cars had all been withdrawn by 1931, so that the brown livery, a relic of horse days, was gone. After a while cars began to appear with 'London Transport' on the side, and stock transfers began which will be detailed later. The LCC had had by far the largest fleet of trams, and it may be that its determination to hold on to a basic design of car from 1907 to 1931 played into the hands of those claiming that tramways were out-dated. True, the borough lines were even more so, but the company lines with their sleek UCC cars (mixed in, it is fair to say, with some pretty old stuff) presented a vision which might have worked against the oil-engined bus lobby – for that was the enemy, and not the trolleybus.

STOCK SUMMARY

Class	Numbers	Date	Wheels	Seats	Body	Trucks	Motors
A	1–100	1903	8	66	Dick, Kerr	2 × Brill 22E	2 × DK3A
—	101	1900	8	—	Milnes	2 × Brill 22E	Westinghouse
B	102–201	1903	4	56	Dick, Kerr	Brill 21E	DK 24A
C	202–301	1905	4	56	Brush	Brill 21E	Westinghouse
D	302–376	1904	8	66	Brush	2 × McGuire	Westinghouse
D	377–401	1905	8	66	B.E.C.	2 × McGuire	Westinghouse
F	552–567	1905	8	36	Dick, Kerr	2 × M&G	DK3A
G	568–601	1906–8	8	36	Brush	2 × M&G	Westinghouse
E	402–551	1906	8	76	Hurst, Nelson	2 × M&G	Westinghouse
	602–751	1907		76	Hurst, Nelson	2 × M&G	Westinghouse
E1	752–1426	1907–10	8	78	Hurst, Nelson LCC	M&G, H&F&HN	2 × 42 hp
E1	1477–1676	1910–11	8	78	Brush	Heenan&Froude	W2 × 42 hp
E1	1727–1776	1920–1	8	78	Hurst, Nelson	HN	MV2 × 60 hp
E1	1777–1851	1921–2	8	78	Brush	HN	DK2 × 60 hp
M	1427–1476	1910	4	62	Hurst, Nelson	HN	Westinghouse
M	1677–1726	1912	4	62	Brush	H&F	W2 × 42 hp
HR1	1852	1929	8	74	LCC	HN	M.V. 109 4 × 35 hp
HR2	1853	1929	8	74	LCC	HN	M.V. 109
HR2	1854–1903	1930	8	74	English Elec.	EMB Co.	M.V. 109
HR2	101–160	1931	8	74	Hurst, Nelson	EMB Co.	M.V. 109
E3	1904–2003	1930	8	74	Hurst, Nelson	EMB Co.	2 × D.K. 126A
E3	161–210	1931	8	74	English Elec.	EMB Co.	2 × BTH 509
—	1	1932	8	66	LCC	EMB Co.	M.V. 109Z

M&G: Mountain & Gibson; DK3A: 37 hp; Westinghouse: 42½ hp; DK126A: 57½ hp; BTH 509: 60 hp.

Class 'H' were watering cars, Nos. 01–04; classes 'J', 'K' and 'L' covered a number of stores vans (05–015). Class 'E2' was an improved 'E1' designed in 1920, but not constructed.

The original experimental bogie car 101 was renumbered 110 in 1921 after being cut down to single-deck; 'B' class No. 110 became 101. In 1933 'M' class No. 1441 became bogie car class 'ME/1' and Nos. 1441/4 were rebuilt as bogie cars class 'ME/3'. No. 1446 was rebuilt to 'E1' and renumbered 1370. 'HR2' class No. 160 was given E3 bogies. In 1933 cars Nos. 835, 1360, were fitted with bow current-collectors and 1172 with pantographs.

The above table indicates equipment on delivery; however there was much replacement of motors, usually to increase power and speed. By 1933

The change-pit at Camberwell seen here in 1949 with the attendant having just guided in the plough with the 'fork' he is carrying, and the conductor is securing the trolley pole.   *H.B. Priestley*

The Hop Exchange (Borough) terminus in 1949. The layout has been simplified to save a switch, the remaining one being spring-loaded as can clearly be seen in this view. There were two routes using this terminal spur near London Bridge station.

H.B. Priestley

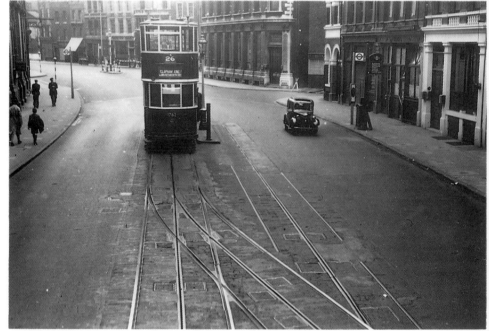

Twin conduits were the simplest way of dealing with a rare instance of single-track on the conduit-operated sections.

A cast-iron LCCT section feeder pedestal, with a telephone to 'control' mounted on top. It contained breaker switches.

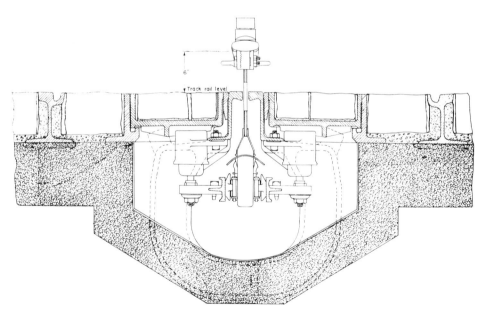

A cross section of the LCCT conduit, showing the 'plough' making contact with power rail and return rail.

motors in use were by Metropolitan Vickers, English Electric, Westinghouse, Dick, Kerr and British Thomson-Houston.

No LCC car was demolished in accidents, it appears, though, that 'B' class No. 110 was heavily damaged when it overturned in Lewisham on 2nd September, 1911. When repaired it became No. 101, the original 101 having by that time taken the number 110.

The only cars sold out of service were 59 'B' class, a war-time effort to provide transport for munition workers on other systems. Twenty went to Sheffield, ten to Rotherham, six to Newport and six to Southampton; also a net 17 cars went to Bexley though there was some coming and going of cars on loan. Three 'B' class trucks were sold to Leyton.

Twenty-one 'B' class and 18 'C' class became snow-brooms, being cut down to single deck. Two 'B' class, Nos. 107 and 158, became staff cars but kept their numbers; they were used up to 1930 to carry workpeople to Charlton depot. Snowbroom No. 045 (former 'C' class No. 215) was still at Brixton depot in 1935. Almost all of them survived until 1950–52, in store, unused.

The 1932 experimental car No. 1 was classed 'HR2' and ran on two EMB trucks; painted blue and white, it is seen here at Mount Pleasant on 6th May, 1933 *en route* to Manor House.   *Author*

Abbey Wood depot in September 1932; the car just visible inside is snow-broom car No. 016.   *Author*

STREET TRAVEL IN GRANDPA'S DAY. Compare the L.C.C. Tramcar of to-day (right) with its forerunners on the left. The steam-drawn tramcar belonged to the 1880's and served Finsbury Park and Edmonton. Passengers on the open top-deck paid smaller fares than those within, because they were exposed not only to wind and rain but to sparks and smoke from the chimney! The horse-drawn tramcar carried the holiday-maker to the Zoo and Hampstead Heath, at a leisurely six miles an hour compared with the electric tramcar's Ten miles an hour to-day, intense street congestion notwithstanding.

SIXTY MORE PULLMAN TRAMCARS, so popular to-day, have been ordered by L.C.C. Tramways and 50 more by Leyton Tramways. So that by March, 1932, an all-Pullman fleet of 1710 tramcars will be in service.

Published by LONDON COUNTY COUNCIL TRAMWAYS, 23 Belvedere Road, S.E. 1.

An advertisement published by the LCCT in 1931 depicting: (top left) a Merryweather steam tram of the North London Suburban Tramways, (below) a London Street Tramways car at Mornington Crescent and (right) a new class 'HR2' tramcar No. 1862.   Author's Collection

A fine detailed view of London United No. 72, a 'Z' class car, at Fulwell depot in 1933. It was built in 1901 on Peckham trucks, and fitted with a top cover about 1911.

London Transport

Chapter Six
The 'Company' Lines

LONDON UNITED TRAMWAYS (LUT)

Following the lifting of Train's tramway down the Bayswater Road, plans were made in 1869 to replace it, and in 1871 an extension was proposed through Shepherds Bush to Southall. The Southall, Ealing & Shepherds Bush Tram-Railway Co. obtained an Act in 1873, and a line was opened in 1876 from Shepherds Bush to Priory Road, Acton. In 1881 a new company was authorised, West Metropolitan Tramways Co., which took control, and intended laying extensions to Hammersmith, Kew Bridge and Richmond. By 1893 the company was bankrupt, having opened these 6½ miles of route. The Richmond line, opened in 1883, was separated from the others by the river. In 1894 the London United Tramways Ltd (LUT) was formed, and took over the lines and stock: 30 horses and six cars at Richmond, 160 horses and 20 cars at Chiswick, and 61 horses and seven cars at Shepherds Bush. J. Clifton Robinson was the Managing Director, and much of the financial backing came from the Imperial Tramways Group in Bristol.

The decision to electrify the system was taken before 1900; Acts for various extensions were obtained, and a Light Railway Order for a line to Uxbridge. The first electric service was opened on 4th April, 1901, from Shepherds Bush to Acton, and Hammersmith and Shepherds Bush to Kew Bridge. There were some problems with electrical interference at Kew Observatory and the opening ceremony was put off until 10th July, at the time another new line was opened, from Acton to Southall.

Up to 1906 all the electric lines were in the County of London or Middlesex, but between then and 1907 eight new routes were opened to the Kingston and Wimbledon areas in Surrey. There was still the isolated route from Richmond to Kew Bridge being worked by horses; powers to electrify were obtained but not used, and the line closed in 1912, because Richmond Council refused to have overhead wires.

As explained later under the MET heading, the LUT became part of the London & Suburban Traction Co. Ltd. under LGOC and Underground control, in close association with British Electric Traction. This group of 'company' lines resulted in the LCC being kept out of West London on the whole, though all the Hammersmith lines were sold to the LCC and there was amicable inter-working; from 1926 LCC cars ran through to Hampton Court. The western boundary of the LCC lines was formed by that running from Wandsworth via Putney, Fulham and Hammersmith to join the MET route from Paddington east of Harlesden. The two main LUT routes west from Shepherds Bush tube station to Acton Vale and Chiswick respectively, crossed over the LCC tracks in Uxbridge Road and Goldhawk Road. The Shepherds Bush junction was a busy one, and later had a system installed whereby the points could be shifted automatically according to whether the approaching car was under power or not.

The LUT experimented with one-man operated cars in 1922 (single deckers) but gave them up in 1928. By 1930 trolleybuses were being seriously considered, and in October 1930 the LUT carried out trials with a six-wheeled trolleybus borrowed from English Electric/GEC. Sixty buses were ordered to be built by the Union Construction Co. Ltd., an Underground Group subsidiary. The first tram service to be turned over to trolleybuses

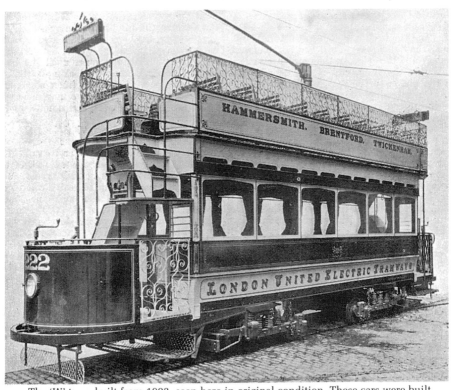

The 'W' type, built from 1902, seen here in original condition. These cars were built
by G.F. Milnes & Co. Ltd. (125) and the British Electric Car Co. Ltd. (25) and ran on
Brill trucks. They differed little in appearance from the 'X' class.

Tramway & Railway World

A 'W' class tramcar *en route* for Hampton Court about 1929. The car behind has
received a top cover and beyond that is a LCCT 'E' class car.   *Lens of Sutton*

was Twickenham to Teddington station on 7th May, 1931, and five routes had been turned over by 2nd September that year. It had been intended to use them on lightly-loaded routes, but after 1933 LPTB took them up with more enthusiasm. The first LUT trolleybuses were somewhat severe in appearance; for some reason they were often called the 'Diddlers'.

After this brief history of the company, it is now time to look at the rolling stock, which differed markedly from that of the LCC, though some types showed a close resemblance to those of the neighbouring MET.

The letter series covering London United tramcars ran backwards, starting at Z. This may have been to avoid any confusion with the cars of the Metropolitan Electric Tramways, and the codes were not allocated until after both companies had come under partially the same ownership in 1913. The 'Z' type of 1901, one hundred of which were ordered, was built by Hurst, Nelson and used normal Peckham bogies; they were open-topped, with six windows to the lower saloon having flat triangle tops, which gave an archaic air, enhanced later when the covered top sported six similar ones. The top deck did not extend over the driver's portion and was flat-fronted, with reversed stairs having a 'landing'. They were fitted with trolley-pole standards and somewhat high intricate ironwork above the top-deck side-panels. The 50 'X' class which followed, built by Milnes, were basically similar, but were carried on McGuire trucks; these also came into service in 1901. The 'W' class of 1902 (150) again was similar, but this time ran on Brill trucks; these were the last of the old-style cars, all double-deckers seating 70, later reduced to 69. Some of the Z types were fitted with top covers and re-designated Y-type; similarly some of the W cars were fitted with top covers and became 'U' type. Five of the W class were given top covers and later more powerful motors, and designted 'WT'. Three U-types were remotored to become 'U2' class. 'W' class No. 175 was rebuilt as a single-deck car with luxury interior, called a 'Social Saloon' for hire, but often to be seen in a siding at Sir Clifton Robinson's home in Hampton.

The 'T' type of 1907, of which only 40 were built, seated 74 and ran on Brill trucks with two 40 hp Westinghouse motors; they had covered tops with open end balconies. These came over the driving position, and this avoided the square body ends which gave earlier types their old-fashioned look. Also the windows were square, with top-lights. As with all the earlier cars, life-guard slats were fitted between the bogies, something the LCC cars could not have because of the plough equipment.

Cars 341–4 were converted in 1922–5 and 342–4 started out as double-deck, but were best known as 32-seat single deckers working as one-man-operated until 1928; No. 341 was type 'S1' and the others 'S2'.

No. 350 was allotted to the 'Poppy' car developed by the LGOC, tried on the MET in 1927 and passed to LUT after a year. It was quite revolutionary in appearance, and only lasted until 1935. A development of it came with the Union Construction Co. cars 351–96 of 1931, usually known as 'Feltham' cars and based on the experimental MET car No. 320 of 1929. They were sleekly streamlined, with a low profile and very comfortable seating for 64 passengers. The LUT version was powered by two 70 hp GEC motors.

London United Tramways vehicle No. 342 was one of three Pay-as-you-enter single deck tramcars built by Milnes in 1902 as DD and converted to SD in 1925. Note the crudely constructed roof clerestory. *London Transport*

This is an advertisement photograph referring to No. 175, known as the 'social saloon'. The vehicle was a cut-down 'W' class, but fitted with luxury seating, often to be seen in a siding at Garrick Villa the residence of Sir Clifton Robinson at Hampton Court. *London Transport*

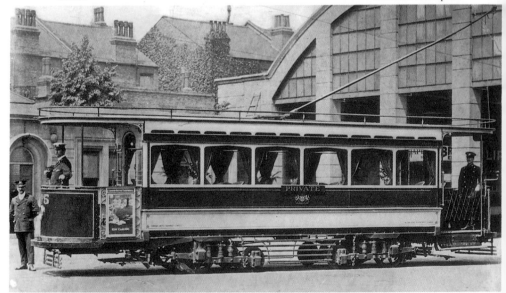

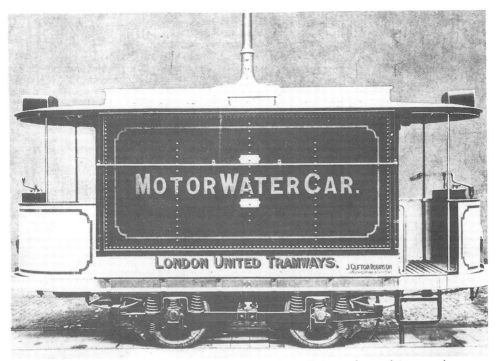

This interesting little service vehicle (Motor Water Car) was featured in an early article in the tramway press extolling the enterprise of London United Tramways.

Author's Collection

LUT No. 332 was a 'T' class tramcar built in 1907 on Brill Trucks and is seen here at Shepherds Bush about 1927 in the standard livery of that time.   *Lens of Sutton*

One of the Feltham cars allotted to the LUT seen here outside Shepherds Bush station on the Southall route. These tramcars were constructed in 1931 by the Union Construction Company.
Lens of Sutton

The 'Poppy' experimental tramcar No. 350 built by the LGOC at Chiswick in 1927 seen here at Gunnersbury station in June 1932 on its way to Hounslow.
Author

One of the first LUT trolley buses, a 'Diddler' seen here at Wimbledon station on 19th January, 1932. Sixty of these buses were built in 1931 by the Union Construction Co., on AEC '663T' chassis.
Author

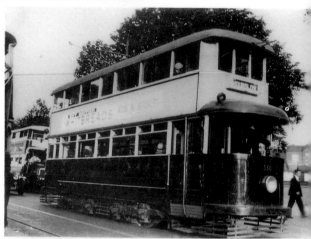

The LUT depots were at Acton, Hillingdon, Hanwell, Fulwell and Hounslow. Livery was at first white, then blue and white, and from about 1925 red and white. Mr Eric Fayne recalled that cars 1 and 161 were in blue livery almost to the end; also that some top covers did not come down to floor level, causing bitter draughts in winter. He also had memories of many tight corners on the system, the worst at Surbiton Park Terrace and Kingston Apple Market. He personally never saw a derailment 'but marks on the road showed that one did occur'.

In the early years cars carried 'London United Electric Tramways' on the turn-under and a monogram on the side; the sides of the top deck bore the names of the principal points of call, e.g. 'Hammersmith, Brentford, Twickenham'.

At one time the LUT were much inconvenienced by flooded roads around Malden, and cars 141/2 were rebuilt for flood service, one with motors above the floor and the other as a trailer.

ROLLING STOCK SUMMARY

Type	Numbers	Date	Wheels	Seats	Body	Trucks	Motors
Z	1–100	1901	8	70	H. Nelson	Peckham	2 × 25 hp
X	101–150	1901	8	70	Milnes	McGuire	2 × 25 hp
W	151–300	1902–4	8	70	Milnes/BEC	Brill	2 × 25 hp
T	301–340	1906	8	74		Brill	2 × 40 hp
S1*	341	1922	8	30	Brush	Brush roll	2 × 25 hp (single deck)
S2†	342–4	1925	8	32	Milnes	Brill	2 × 25 hp (single deck)
Poppy	350	1927	8	64	LGOC	Brush	BTH 2 × 50 hp
UCC	351–396	1931	8	64	UC Co.	EMB	2 × 70 hp

BEC Co.: British Electric Car Co. UCC: Union Construction Co. Ltd.
No. 175 (class 'W') converted to s.d. saloon.
*Built 1905, purchased 1922;   †Built 1901 as D.D., converted 1925.

METROPOLITAN ELECTRIC TRAMWAYS (MET)

The area later served by the MET was somewhat sparsely populated when horse tramways were being developed south of the river, and the original termini of the North Metropolitan at Highgate, Finsbury Park, Manor House and Stamford Hill remained the limit. However, the North London Suburban Tramway Co. did get a tramways Order in 1879 for a line from Stamford Hill to Ponders End, opened 1881–2, converted in 1884 to steam traction. The addition of a line to Wood Green in 1887 brought the need for rolling stock up to 25 engines and 27 bogie cars. However traffic was thin and in January 1890 the company was wound up; the whole thing was sold to the North Met, which reverted to horse traction on the lines.

In November 1894 the Metropolitan Tramways and Omnibus Co. was formed, from 1899 associated with British Electric Traction, and some 50 miles of tramways were planned, in collaboration with the Middlesex and Herts County Councils. In 1902 the company became the Metropolitan Electric Tramways Co. and bought all the former steam lines from Northmet, together with 62 cars and 625 horses, leaving the latter with 48 miles of other

SOME UNFULFILLED LONDON TRAMWAY SCHEMES

All these horse steam & cable tramway proposals were submitted to Parliament. Some were authorised, but none constructed. There were many others, chiefly in the inner areas, which cannot conveniently be shown on a scale as small as this.	Chesham Boxmoor & Hemel Hempstead Steam Tr'ys.	C 1888	11·09	3′-6″
	Highgate Finchley and Barnet Tramways (cable)	A 1885	6·45	do
	West Metropolitan Tramways Company Extensions (horse)	1883	8·33	4′-8½
	Southall Ealing & Shepherds Bush Tram-Railway Co Ltd.	G 1871	7·05	do
	Uxbridge Southall and Brentford Tramway Company (h's)	G 1872	9½	?
	Brentford and Isleworth Tramway Company (horse)	1879	1·13	4′-8½
	Staines and Egham Tramways (steam) (P to Q on map)	C 1887	3·37	3′-6″
	Kew Richmond and Kingston-on-Thames Tramways (horse)	1872	6·69	?
	Kingston and Surbiton Tramways Company (horse)	1883	5·56	3′-6″

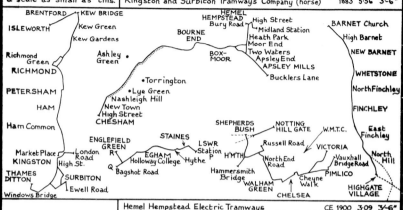

These proposals for electric tramways were submitted to Parliament or the L.R.C. but all were withdrawn or rejected. Certain other proposals, some of which were later authorised in another form, are not shown. Proposals which were authorised, also the proposals of established operators, are shown on the main map, but the latter are not in the mileage statistics.	Hemel Hempstead Electric Tramways	CE 1900	3·09	3′-6″
	Hem. Hemp. Trys; Metropolitan Tramways & Omnibus Co Ltd.	DE 1900	3·45	4′-8½
	Tottenham & Epping Forest Light Rlys (M.T.&O.)	DH 1901	10	do
	Finchley Hendon & District Lt Rlys (Electric) Co Ltd.	BJ 1898	9	3′-6″
	Finchley District Electric Traction Co Ltd	B 1900	26	4′-8½
	Finchley and Hendon Tramways Company. (C.C.E.H.Rly)	1901	5·15	do
	Finchley Urban District Council Tramways	K 1901	4·00	do
	Willesden Urban District Council Tramways	F 1901	5·09	do
	Ealing Urban District Council Tramways	F 1900	2·05	do
	Chiswick Urban District Council Tramways	1902	4·66	do
	Richmond Electric Light & Power Co Ltd	1908	8·05	do
	Hounslow & Twickenham Light Railways (Drake & Gorham)	1899	6¾	3′-6″
	Staines and Egham Light Railway Co Ltd (P to R)	1900	3½	do
	Metropolitan District Electric Traction Co Ltd (M.D.Rly)	1901	24¼	4′-8½
	Kingston Surbiton & District Light Railway Company	1900	11·20	do
	Kingston Urban District Council Tramways	1900	5·98	do
	Surbiton Urban District Council Tramways	1900	4·32	do
	Wimbledon Urban District Council Tramways	1901	1·94	do
	Coulsdon Urban District Council Tr'ys (S to T on map)	1904	3·92	do
	Croydon & Southern Districts Tramways Co (S to U).	C 1908	4·20	do
	London Southern Tramways Company (electric)	L 1898	12	do

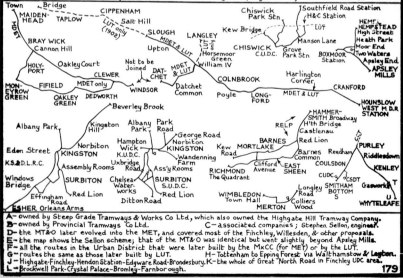

A — owned by Steep Grade Tramways & Works Co Ltd, which also owned the Highgate Hill Tramway Company.
B — owned by Provincial Tramways Co Ltd.   C — associated companies ; Stephen Sellon, engineer.
D — the MT&O later evolved into the MET, and covered most of the Finchley, Willesden, & other proposals.
E — the map shows the Sellon scheme; that of the MT&O later went slightly beyond Apsley Mills.
F — all the routes in the Urban District that were later built by the MxCC (for MET) or by the LUT.
G — routes the same as those later built by LUT.   H — Tottenham to Epping Forest via Walthamstow & Leyton.
J — Highgate-Finchley-Hendon Station-Edgware Road-Brondesbury. K — the whole of Great North Road in Finchley UDC area.
L — Brockwell Park-Crystal Palace-Bromley-Farnborough.

179

horse tramways, which were sold to LCC or West Ham or Leyton. Only a small portion of the originally-planned MET routes came to fruition, but more were progressively obtained, a small one being the Harrow Road & Paddington Co. of 1886, taken over in 1904, and electrified in 1906.

The first electric route was opened on 22nd July, 1904, from Finsbury Park to Wood Green. A boundary had been agreed with the London United Tramways immediately south of the Harrow Road, and the Acton–Harlesden line, part of the Middlesex County Light Railways, was to be leased to LUT, but taken back in 1905 when a new boundary was fixed north of Uxbridge Road. It did not in fact open until 1909. Other small sections had to be sold to the LCC under statutory powers; there were five places where the MET and LCCT met.

In 1912 British Electric Traction promoted a scheme to consolidate the interests of MET, LUT and a recently formed Tramways (MET) Omnibus Co., and the London & Suburban Traction Co. Ltd was formed for this purpose. Shortly after, an agreement was made with the London General Omnibus Co. that the MET buses would work with them; a small fleet of buses operated under the 'Southern' name by SMET was also taken in in 1913. In 1912 the LGOC became part of the 'Underground' Group, and in 1914 it was decided that the Group would take over L & ST Co. also. Although BET still had a large financial interest, in effect the 'Company' lines had joined a large monopoly.

Perhaps because of the Group's pre-occupation with buses and railways, the MET trams showed little development until 1926, when the permitted speed was increased from 16 to 20 mph, and next year two experimental cars were built, 'Bluebell' at Hendon works, and 'Poppy' at the LGOC Chiswick works. Many cars were given upholstered seats and more powerful motors. In 1929 the famous 'Feltham' cars started to come into service, sleekly streamlined luxury cars of which 100 were built by a Group subsidiary, the Union Construction Co. Ltd up to 1931; 54 were given to MET and 46 to LUT.

Of the 316 MET cars, 22 were still open-top and 15 single-deck; 160 were equipped with ploughs, as the MET was now running over various LCC connections and also used the conduit on its route to Holborn terminus. There were depots at Wood Green, Edmonton, Finchley, Hendon and Stonebridge Park. The North Finchley depot was especially well-equipped, cars being moved mainly by traversers; a car could be washed outside and vacuumed inside in five minutes.

The MET car list consisted of a huge total of 316 cars; it began with two types built in 1904/5, 'A' and 'B'; however the 'B'-type took the first 70 numbers, and the 'A'-type 71–130. Both were open-top bogie cars, class 'A' very similar to the first LUT cars, and class 'B' looking less archaic because the top deck was carried fully over the driver's platform and the front of the top deck was not flat. Right-angle stairs with landings were fitted to class 'A', and the Brush trucks on both types with the small wheels leading seemed strange to people used to LCC cars. Class 'A', also 'E' and 'G' carried 'County Council of Middlesex' on the side panels and all types had 'Metropolitan Electric Tramways Ltd.' on the turn-under. Later only a monogram

This commercial postcard states 'New Electric Car'. The MET 'A' class came out in 1904, built and trucked by Brush. Note the trucks with pony wheels at the outer ends, also the wire life-guards at the ends and between the trucks.   *Lens of Sutton*

No. 202 of The Metropolitan Electric Tramways was a 'C1' class car built in 1909 and is seen here as it passes through The Broadway, Hendon on its way to Canons Park about 1910.   *Lens of Sutton*

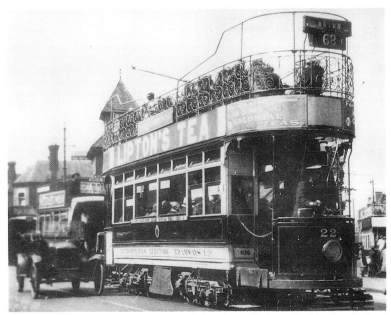

The 'B' class, of which No. 22 was one, differed greatly from the 'A' class in having square windows and round instead of square ends, although both types came out in 1904/5. It is seen here on the Wembley to Acton route about 1927. Note the very ornate ironwork around the upper deck. *Lens of Sutton*

Single-deck MET E-type car No. 148, built in 1905 on a Brush radial truck, photographed on the Alexandra Palace route near its junction with the line down Tottenham High Road at Bruce Grove. *Lens of Sutton*

On the back of this photograph taken inside Wood Green Depot is written: 'Taken by Frost-Smith end of 1907 or early 1908.' P.H. Frost-Smith had been with BET but left to become a prime mover in petrol electric transport. Note the patching metal work on the front of No. 82, 'A' class showing that the headlight had been moved from the dashboard position to the upper deck position, the normal position for MET trams for many years.

Author's Collection

was used on the side panels. The early cars carried the headlight on the front of the top deck and not on the driver's apron. Sixteen of the 'B' type were top-covered later and designated 'B2'. Type 'A' were all top-covered later.

Twenty four-wheeled cars, Nos. 131–150, came out in 1905, a single-deck version of the 'A' type, seating 36. Only 15 of these 'E' type lasted to 1933 as some were sold, four going to Auckland, New Zealand, and one to the LVT. The Brush trucks were of the radial type.

The next bogie type was the 'C', Nos. 151–165, 74-seaters similar to the 'B' cars, but with top-lights above the windows of the saloon. They were open-topped, but fitted with full-length covers, leaving verandahs, in 1912 –16 thus becoming class C2. The top deck ends were fully-rounded over the driver's position. The Brush trucks were given 40 hp high-speed motors in 1912 and 50 hp in 1927. This class, and the 'D' class, both came out in 1906; the latter were 25 four-wheelers, and one extra car, No. 191, class D1, was acquired from Leicester. They seated 54, quite normal for a non-bogie car. They gave very good service until 1931, when they were replaced by the new and much larger Feltham cars.

The 'C1' class of 1909 (Nos. 192–211) were again open-top bogie cars, which did not get their top covers until 1929; the original Mountain & Gibson bogies were given BT-H high-speed motors in 1929. The 'F' class of the same year seated 78 and always had top-covers. The 'G' type of the same year was the last to be delivered with open tops. One of these, No. 317, was a late build in 1922. Type 'H' was a large class, 80 cars built from 1909 to 1912, and six more in 1925–6. These cars retained the Tudor Arch-topped windows to the saloon, but with top lights. All of them always had fully-enclosed top decks. The seating of 78 was reduced to 74 when transver seats were fitted in 1928–30. Types 'F' to 'H' all had M&G trucks, and were all remotored with BT-H high-speed motors in 1929–30. All had their trucks mounted with the driving wheels outwards.

The 'Bluebell' car of 1927, No. 318, represented an overdue attempt at a modern-looking car; it had 8 windows to the saloon and 10 to the top; the driver's cab was enclosed, and at first it had air brakes, though later magnetic ones were fitted. It was built at the MET Hendon works; it first came out with a flat roof, replaced later with a higher domed roof. The search for the perfect car continued; No. 320 and 330 by UCC with Met-Vick and B.T.-H. motors came in 1929, and 331 with centre-entrance and four GEC motors. Finally the standard 64-seat 'Feltham' car was produced in 1931, with end-doors and BT-H 70 hp motors. Fifty-four were built for MET and 46 for LUT. They were too good to scrap, and twenty years later most went off for further life at Leeds.

It is of interest that up to 1931 one could still travel on an open-top four wheeler into the centre of London (Aldersgate Street) on a 'D' class car working route 51 from Muswell Hill.

The MET pioneered the trolley-bus in London, with a BT-H single-deck car which ran inside the Hendon depot as an experiment in 1909. It was not then followed up.

'H' type No. 245 of 1909 seen at Holborn Terminus in October 1932. This tramcar (courtesy of the LCC) had worked down from Edmonton (via Manor House) (where the overhead pick-up was changed to the plough) and the Caledonian Road.   *Author*

The 'Bluebell' experimental tramcar of 1927, No. 318 as remodelled in 1929 with the domed roof. Note the way in and way out signs and the attractive Palmolive soap advert. Photographed at Finchley Depot.   *London Transport*

A UCC 'Feltham' tramcar of 1931; this one carries a notice 'Passengers Alight Front End', but most cars had a similar notice 'Passengers Alight Front and Rear End'.

London Transport

Tramway accidents varied from a bent dash to full-scale disaster; here an MET 'A' class has left the track and overturned. This photograph appeared in the *Morning Post* of 6th November, 1929.

This 'J' class SMET tram, running on Lycett & Conaty radial truck by Brush, was taken either on the Anerley Hill braking tests on 10th April, 1906, or when this end of the route opened to the public on 28th May, 1906.   *Lens of Sutton*

First Tramcar, Anerley Hill.

ROLLING STOCK SUMMARY

Type	Numbers	Date	Wheels	Seats	Body	Trucks	Motors
B	1–70	1904	8	68	Brush	Brush	2 × 28 hp
A	71–130	1904	8	68	Brush	Brush	2 × 28 hp
E	131–150	1905	4	36	Brush	Brush (radial)	2 × 28 hp
C	151–165	1907	8	74	Brush	Brush	2 × 28 hp
D	166–191	1907	4	54	Brush	Brush (radial)	2 × 28 hp
C1	192–211	1909	8	74	Brush	M&G	2 × 28 hp
F	212–216	1909	8	78	Brush	M&G	2 × 28 hp
G	217–236	1909	8	74	Brush	M&G	2 × 40 hp
G	317	1922	8	74	Brush	M&G	2 × 50 hp
H	237–316	1909–12	8	78	Brush	M&G/Brush	2 × 40 hp
H	2, 12, 22, 31, 46, 82	1925–6	8	73	Brush	Brush	2 × 60 hp
Bluebell	318	1927	8	71	MET	Brush	2 × 50 hp
UCC	320	1929	8	64	UC Co.	MV	4 × 35 hp
UCC	330	1929	8	62	UC Co.	Brush	2 × 50 hp
UCC	331	1930	8	70	UC Co.	UCC	4 × 35 hp
	319, 321–9, 332–375	1931	8	64	UC Co.	EMB	2 × 70 hp

Nos. 131–150 were single deck. 16 B class cars top-covered became B2, but all A cars were top-covered remaining A, 70 seats. All C class top-covered becoming C2, 70 seats. All G top-covered, still 74 seats. No. 132 was fitted with Warner truck (radial) and transferred to LUT. Most of the cars between   and 316 later received new higher power motors. UCC 330 PAYE, 331 centre-entrance.

SOUTH METROPOLITAN ELECTRIC TRAMWAYS (SMET)

The full title was South Metropolitan Electric Tramways & Lighting Co. Ltd, and the company was formed in 1904 to run to the Croydon boundary from Penge, Crystal Palace, Tooting and Sutton. In fact, the tramways always lost money and it was the lighting supply side which kept the company going. It became part of the Underground Group on 1st January, 1913, when the route mileage was 13.08 miles, or 15¾ if through running was included. At Tooting Junction a connection was put in with the LCCT.

The first line to open was along Penge Road to the Thicket Road terminus, and from the 'Robin Hood', Croydon Road, to Low Level station, on 12th April, 1906; a steep extension up Anerley Hill did not open until 28th May as not enough experienced drivers for hill working were available. The important Mitcham route opened on 24th May the same year; Sutton was reached on 10th August.

The line started with 16 type 'J' cars (1–16) built by United Electric Car Co. on long-wheelbase 4-wheel Brush/Lycett & Conaty radial trucks in 1906. In the same year Nos. 17–26 were taken over from the BET working of the Croydon Corporation system, being 1902 4-wheel Milnes cars (36–45); No. 19 was heavily damaged when it turned over in Wallington on 1st April, 1907, but seems to have survived. Type 'L' were also ex-Croydon, but bogie cars on Brill trucks (former Nos. 56–60) run with the non-driving axles at the outer ends. There were five of these, and four type 'O' bogie cars were obtained from Gravesend Tramways (also 1902 cars); these two types occupied Nos. 27–35. Sixteen new 4-wheel cars of type 'M' obtained in the same year were Nos. 36–51. Type 'P' were four-wheelers from Croydon

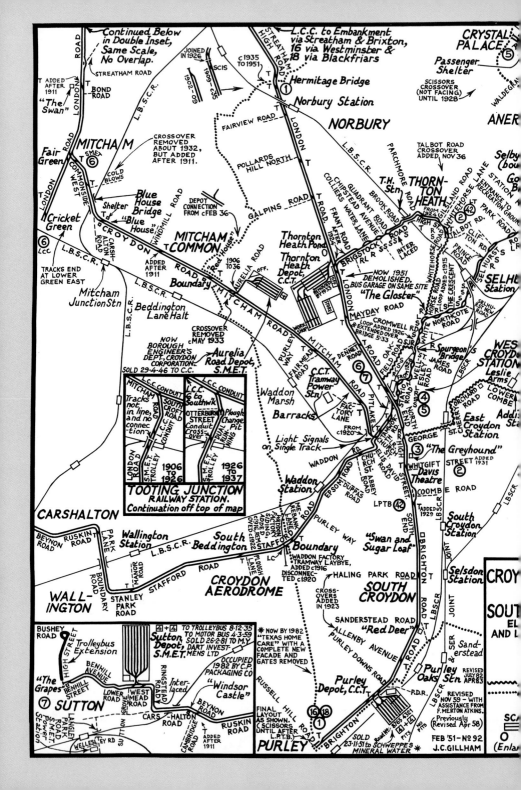

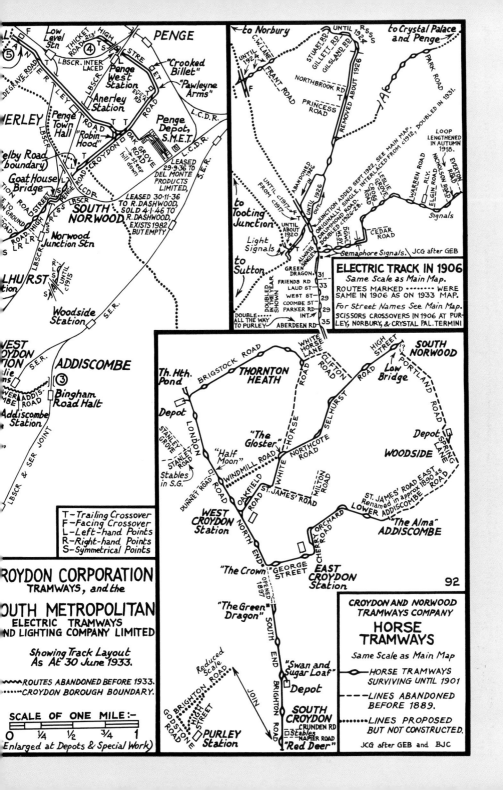

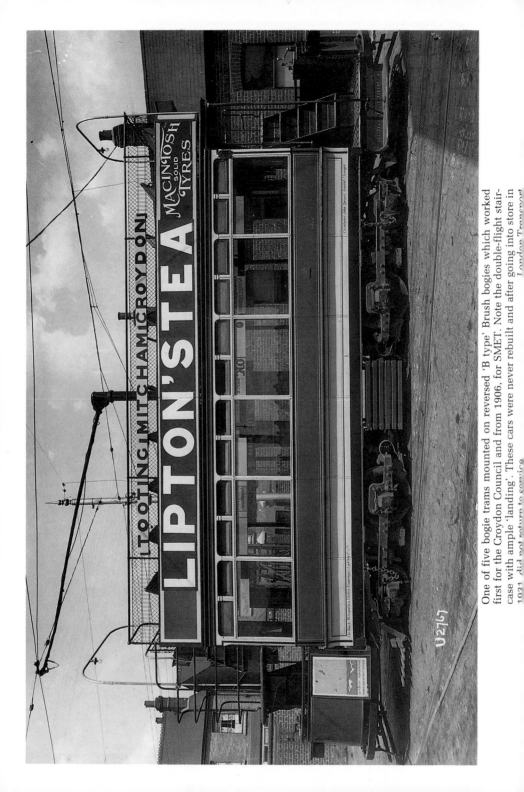

One of five bogie trams mounted on reversed 'B type' Brush bogies which worked first for the Croydon Council and from 1906, for SMET. Note the double-flight staircase with ample 'landing'. These cars were never rebuilt and after going into store in 1921 did not return to service.

SMET Type 'M' car No. 50 was built by Brush in 1906, with Brush 21E-type 7½ ft trucks. It is here seen in June 1932 crossing the railway bridge at Anerley station, towards the Croydon Road. *Author*

In 1931 SMET borrowed ten LUT U-type top-covered bogie cars, built by G.F. Milnes in 1902; the top-cover dates from 1911. No. 269 is seen here at Mitcham Fair Green in January 1932. This route (SMET 6) was of double track all the way from the junction at Church Street in Croydon. *Author*

An SMET 'J' type car in Stafford Road, Waddon, about 1920; note the large Lycett & Conaty axle-boxes, later replaced by Warner boxes.

Lens of Sutton

A 'J' type car in Carshalton on the Sutton route (No. 7), which was double-track all the way from the London Road line, and had the Sutton depot not far from its terminus at 'The Grapes', Sutton; view dating from about 1920. *Lens of Sutton*

The second No. 1 on the Gravesend & Northfleet system, seen here in 1926 at the 'Prince of Orange' terminus of the Windmill Street branch, was one of a batch of four brought in to replace the original bogie cars which were found to be too large for the traffic. *Eric Fayne*

The Gravesend & Northfleet trams were replaced in 1929 by 16 Leyland Titan buses; they ran in tramway livery but were numbered with the Maidstone & District fleet; this is No. 301, at Northfleet in September 1931. *Author*

Corporation which were not acquired until July 1927, and took No. 52 and numbers of three scrapped cars. The 'J' cars had their Conaty radial boxes replaced by Warner type.

Finally in September 1931 ten cars of LUT type 'U' were taken on loan, keeping their LUT numbers. They could not pass on bends on the Sutton–Croydon line.

The Underground Group's prototype trolleybus was tested on the SMET in 1922, before going on to the LUT. Trolleys brought the end of trams on SMET routes, all having been turned over by 12th September, 1937. However the cars themselves did not last that long; though allotted numbers by LPTB they never carried them, though some 'J' and 'M' cars ran for a while with an S suffix.

The SMET livery was green in the early years, later red and white. Depots were at Sutton and Penge.

ROLLING STOCK SUMMARY

Type	Numbers	Date	Wheels	Trucks	
J	1–16	1906	4	Brush/Conaty	New
K	17–26	(1906)	4	Milnes 'girder'	ex-Croydon
L	27–29, 31, 35	(1906)	8	Brush 'B'	ex-Croydon
O	30, 32–4	(1906)	8	Brill 22E	ex-Gravesend
M	36–51	1906	4	Brush 21E	New
P	17, 21, 47, 52	(1930)	4	Brill 21E	ex-Croydon

Dates in brackets are dates of acquisition by SMET.

Six M-type cars (Nos. 37/8, 41/3/6/8) were rebuilt in 1929 with higher dashes and wider top decks, and had a more modern appearance.

Type 'M' cars had specially powerful motors for the West Croydon–Crystal Palace route.

THE GRAVESEND & NORTHFLEET ELECTRIC TRAMWAYS LIMITED

Gravesend in north-west Kent was fortunate enough to have a horse-tramway; it is not surprising when one recalls that the south bank of the Thames here was lined with cement, brick and paper works. It was of narrow (3 ft 6 in.) gauge and opened in 1883, running from Gravesend Clock Tower to the Leather Bottle inn at Northfleet; it had only five cars, of a standard type with five windows and garden seats on the top deck. It was titled the Gravesend, Rosherville and Northfleet Tramways Company Limited; the noted Rosherville Gardens west of Gravesend were then still open and provided some traffic.

As related earlier, in 1889 the Series Electric Co. extended the line for ¾ of a mile to Station Road, Northfleet, and the horse-trams used this extension after the electrical trials, the terminus being known as Huggens College. The line was purchased by BET in 1900 and converted to standard gauge, as well as extended to Craylands Lane, Swanscombe. There were also branch lines along Windmill Street, Pelham Road, and the Dover Road.

The first order for 10 bogie trams and 10 four-wheelers, turned out to be excessive, and from 1904 the bogie trams were transferred to other BET

lines, four to SMET, four to Swansea and two to Jarrow. Smaller cars were brought in, all by Brush, Nos. 5/6 from Jarrow and 7/8 from Taunton.

Nos. 5 and 6 were quite small, with single doors to the saloons. Nos. 9 and 10 were 'demi-cars', known locally as 'rabbit hutches' and were only used on the branch lines. They disappeared early, and were replaced by Nos. 7 and 8. No. 7 was a peculiar car, having three saloons and two outside seats on the platforms at each end; it was normally boarded at the front.

Cars 15–20 were given covered tops with open ends, made locally at Dartford. These cars had reversed stairways, whereas the replacements for the bogie cars had normal ones. The livery was brown and cream up to 1921, then red and cream; however car No. 1 was at one time painted white and advertised Russell's Brewery.

The trams were replaced by a fleet of 16 Leyland Titan buses with open stair-cases but covered tops, painted in tramway livery but numbered in with Maidstone & District's fleet (298–313).

ROLLING STOCK SUMMARY

Numbers	Date	Wheels	Origin	Body	Trucks
(1–10)	1902	8	New	Dick, Kerr	Brill
11–20	1902	4	New	Dick, Kerr	Brill
9–10	1904	4*	New	Brush	Brush
1–4	1907	4	New	Brush	Brush
5–6	1910	4	Jarrow	Brush (small)	Brush
7–8	1921	4*	Taunton	Brush	Brush

*single-deck, 5–6 built 1906, 7–8 built, 1905.

One of Dartford Council's cars 'posing' outside the Bull Hotel before the official opening. This was the junction with the Victoria Road branch (*behind the camera*) and the Wilmington branch (*off to left*). All the Dartford cars, which were destroyed in a fire in 1917, were four-wheelers mounted on Brill trucks.   *Author's Collection*

Chapter Seven
The Minicipal Lines South of the River

BEXLEY COUNCIL TRAMWAYS AND DARTFORD LIGHT RAILWAY

Bexley Urban District Council was early in the tramway race, promoting a Bill in 1901 for a line to Plumstead, where the existing horse-tramways ended, from Bexleyheath. The Urban and Rural Councils of Dartford were to apply for a line joining it at the District boundary at Gravel Hill, but finding that a Tramway Order could not be made for a rural council, successfully applied for a Light Railway Order, which with a subsequent addition took the tramway to Horns Cross, a lonely spot east of Dartford near Stone. A talked-of further extension of 1½ miles would have brought it to join the Gravesend system at its terminus at Craylands Lane, Swanscombe, but this was not done. The Dartford system had two short branches, from the Bull Hotel to Wilmington and to Victoria Road, where the depot was built. The Bexley system opened on 3rd October, 1903, and the Dartford one on 14th February, 1906, worked by contractors J.G. White & Co. Bexley also had a branch line, from Market Place to Northumberland Heath, where there was an end-on junction with the Erith system. At first the boundaries were respected, and Dartford cars terminated at Gravel Hill, but soon it was seen as more expedient for Dartford to work to Market Place, and for Erith to do likewise, over Bexley metals from Northumberland Heath.

Meanwhile the LCC was reconstructing the tramway from Plumstead (Plume of Feathers) to Beresford Square near the Arsenal at Woolwich, having taken over the narrow gauge Woolwich & South-east London Tramways in 1905. On 18th June, 1908 the Bexley service was extended to Beresford Square.

After the outbreak of war in 1914 special arrangements had to be made for the workers at the many munitions factories in the area; Bexley cars were allowed to work over Dartford track to the Vickers Crayford works; it is said that five 'E1' class cars were hired from the LCC for this work.

Dartford had started with 12 cars in a livery of maroon and yellow, built by UEC on Brill 4-wheeled trucks; to cope with extra traffic one of the Erith 'demi-cars' had been purchased and numbered 13. Unfortunately in August 1917 the entire fleet was destroyed in a fire at the depot. In view of the serious need for maintaining service to the factories, Bexley purchased 17 and hired a further six 'B' class cars from the LCC, which Bexley then operated on behalf of Dartford; some were repainted in Bexley livery and some not. In April 1921 Bexley and Dartford formed a Joint Committee, which then worked the 16 ex-Bexley and 17 ex-LCC cars as one undertaking until 1933. Cars were numbered in the Bexley list as high as 39; however in 1919 six were being returned, and the total actually purchased was 17; numbers were juggled to get a series of 'B' class cars from 17 to 33. This fleet of 33 cars covered all Bexley and Dartford requirements, the open top originals and closed top 'Bs' being used indiscriminately on all workings.

When LPTB took over in 1933, the track on the Dartford part was in a bad state; the Board made some improvements and brought in 12 'M' class cars and two from West Ham, all the original cars having been taken out of service by the end of 1933. The lines did not last long, being replaced on 23rd November, 1935 by trolleybuses, except Dartford–Horns Cross which was bus-served, as also was Wilmington.

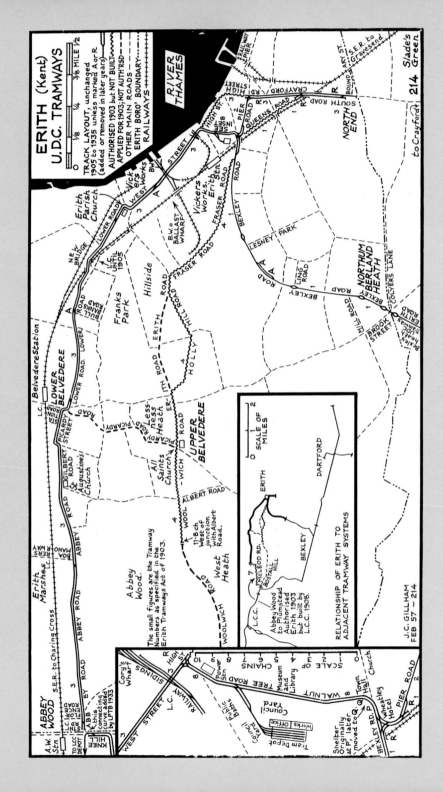

BEXLEY AND DARTFORD JOINT STOCK

Numbers	Date	Wheels	Seats	Body	Trucks	Motors
1–16	1903–4	4	52	Dick, Kerr†	Brush*	Dick, Kerr 25A
17–33	(1917–8)	4	60	Dick, Kerr‡	Brill 21E	Dick, Kerr 25A

*replaced in 1913 by Peckham 'pendulum' type trucks, †open top, ‡covered.

ERITH URBAN DISTRICT COUNCIL

Owing to the establishment in Erith before 1900 of munition factories, there was a call for a new power station, which led naturally to consideration of electric tramways. Several routes were proposed, and a connection with the LCC system at Abbey Wood, though the latter undertaking was not keen. On 26th August, 1905 the system was opened, with a line running from Abbey Wood via Erith to an end-on connection with the Bexley Council line at Northumberland Heath. The section north of Erith station had two level crossings; one with the standard gauge Upper Ballast Wharf branch from the SECR with a narrow gauge line from Parish's Loam Pits beside it, and another SECR siding to Lower Ballast (Station) Wharf. These were awkward to work and expensive to maintain. There was also a crossing for Cory's Wharf in West Street. A branch tramway from Erith to North End was opened on the same day, closed soon after, and then re-opened using Pay-as-you-Enter single deck (or demi-) cars. From July 1908 Erith cars ran through to Bexleyheath Market Place over Bexley metals. Service on the North End route ceased in 1910. The War brought some strain, and cars had to be hired from Leyton and LUT, and in 1916 a car was bought from Hull. After the War, losses were made, services reduced, and bus competition became serious. The cars in their now-drab livery stumbled on until 1933, when the LPTB combined the Erith system with the Bexley one, and closed Erith down on 9th and Bexley on 23rd November, 1935.

The Board had put in a connection at Abbey Wood, in 1933; a consumation which was much desired by the Erith Council for 30 years, during which several meetings had seemed to be near to an agreement for an Erith–Woolwich service, but the cup was always dashed. The Erith line was all double from the junction with the North End route at Pier Road to Abbey Wood; there were five passing places between the junction and the borough boundary at Northumberland Heath. The depot and offices lay on a short branch in Walnut Tree Road, south of High Street. This was closed down by LPTB before the system was.

Livery was originally pea-green and pale yellow, later dark red and white.

ROLLING STOCK SUMMARY

Numbers	Date	Wheels	Seats	Body	Trucks	Motors
1–14	1905	4	52	Brush	M&G 21 EM	2 × 30 hp
(15/16)	1906	4	20	Milnes Voss	M&G	2 × 27 hp
15–18	(1916)	8	74	Milnes	Brill 22E	2 × 30 hp
19	(1916)	8	76	Milnes	Brill 22E	2 × 40 hp

Bexley car No. 11, one of the original 1903 Dick Kerr trams with Peckham trucks seen here at Northumberland Heath in 1930. Normally the Erith car behind would run-through on Bexley metals to Bexleyheath Market Place, but road repairs to the loop had necessitated a shuttle service from here to the Market Place.   *Author*

Bexley tramcar No. 1 in 1932 seen here in Crayford Way running to Woolwich. Note the reversed staircases on these cars.   *Author*

One of the Erith Council tramcars which did not receive a top cover, photographed at Bexleyheath Market Place in January 1932.   *Author*

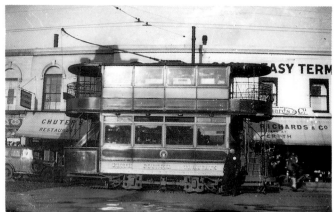

At the same point and date as the previous view, car No. 10 (this time with its covered top) running on Bexley Council track. *Author*

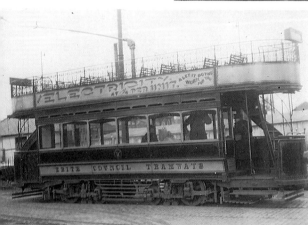

The large ex-LUT bogie car, No. 14 of Erith Council Tramways seen at Walnut Tree Avenue depot in September 1932. *Author*

Croydon Council car No. 13 (class 'W1') passing SMET rebuilt 'M' type car No. 38 in Penge Road, 1932. The SMET car is bound for the Crystal Palace (via Anerley) and the other for West Croydon station. This was one of eighteen loops on the single-line from Selby Road Boundary to West Croydon. *Author*

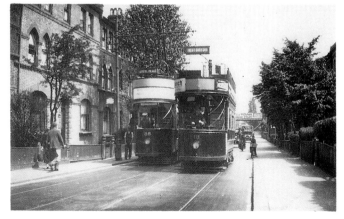

The original 15/16 were 'demi-cars'; one was sold to Dartford and one to Doncaster. New 15–18 were ex-LUT 'W1' cars 187, 192, 221, 252. Nos. 1–6, 9, and the LUT cars remained open-top; 19 (ex-Hull) was covered top on arrival. 19, later 20, was a sweeping car.

COUNTY BOROUGH OF CROYDON

The first trams in the Borough were horse-cars running from Thornton Heath to North End, which started on 9th October, 1879. The Tramway Company bought five Starbuck cars, single-deck, though it was decided almost at once to purchase some double-deck cars with 'knifeboard' seating on the roof, as was then the custom; the metal stairway or ladder leading to the roof was somewhat vertiginous; ladies did not normally use them, though later 'decency boards' were fitted along the sides of the top decks in case they did so. The next line to open, from the 'Green Dragon' to the 'Red Deer' in South Croydon, on 14th May, 1880, could not be joined to the first section because the High Street was too narrow.

Besides the two above, other lines were opened from Thornton Heath (where the depot was sited) to White Horse Lane, West Croydon station to South Norwood, and from George Street to Addiscombe past East Croydon station; an extension to Portland Road, South Norwood, did not last long. The Croydon & Norwood Tramways Co. was an amalgamation in 1883 of the previously separate Croydon and Norwood Co's. A new company was formed in 1890, and experimented with battery-electric cars as mentioned earlier. In 1898 the Croydon Council decided to take over the tramways, and closed the gap along the High Street between the two sections. However it found itself incapable of working the lines, and leased them to BET. It was also decided to electrify, and this work was entrusted to British Thomson-Houston, who worked in co-operation with BET.

The track was entirely relaid and a new depot opened at Purley Downs Road; 35 four-wheeled cars were ordered from G.F. Milnes & Co., who had taken over from Starbuck. The public opening was on 26th September, 1901, though some horse-cars continued for a time.

The rolling stock records are somewhat confused, as for a time some cars were owned by the Council and some by BET. The position up to 1906 was:

Nos. 1–15, 4w. on Peckham trucks 1901 owned by Council
Nos. 18–35 4w. on Brill 21E trucks 1901 owned by Council
Nos. 36–45 4w. by Milnes, Milnes trucks, owned by BET
Nos. 46–55 8w. by Milnes, Brill 22E trucks, 10 owned by Council, 5 by BET 1902
Nos. 56–60 8w. by Brush, Brush B trucks, owned by BET 1902.

In 1906 it was decided to remove the BET cars, which were transferred to South Metropolitan, in which BET had an interest. They were replaced by new 4-wheelers:

Nos. 36–45 (2nd) built by Brush, Mountain & Gibson trucks 1906
Nos. 56–60 (2nd) built by Brush, Mountain & Gibson trucks 1906
Nos. 61–70 (2nd) built by Brush, Brill 21E trucks 1907
Nos. 71–75 (2nd) built by Brush, Brill 21E trucks 1911

In 1927 twelve of these cars were sold to SMET, and the remainder numbered 1–20. Nos. 21–30 were the 1902 bogie cars, and a new series 31–55 was built by Hurst Nelson, similar to the LCCT 'E1' class. They had two GEC 65 hp motors and were designed for the through service from Purley to the Embankment, which was now possible since a 6-inch gap had been filled in at Norbury separating the two systems.

Cars were classified as 'W/1' for 4-wheelers, 'B/1' for old bogie cars, and 'E1' for the new bogie cars, but these did not appear on the sole bars.

The livery for electric cars was originally lake and ivory, and from 1927 dark red and pale grey. 'Croydon Corporation Tramways' appeared on the lower panels.

Bexley car No. 24, a former LCCT 'B' class tramcar purchased in 1917 seen here running east near Crayford in 1931.
Author

The City of London's only tramway was that across Blackfriars Bridge and along the Embankment as far as the Temple Steps, opened on 9th September, 1909, and this was leased to the LCCT. In this view (about 1912) the 'E1' class tramcar looks a bit lonely, but there were also approx. 15 routes using the bridge in 1912 in this picture. Most routes being circular. The bridge had to be widened to take the tram tracks. From the left turn at the far (north) end the trams were on reserved tracks as far as Westminster Bridge; there were no bus routes along the Embankment.

Author's Collection

Chapter Eight
The Municipal Lines North of the River

WEST HAM CORPORATION TRAMWAYS

West Ham was the biggest of the municipal undertakings apart from the LCC, contributing 48 million passenger journeys per annum in 1918. The nucleus of the system was certain lines of the old North-Met, acquired by an Act of 1898; but some additional mileage was also constructed. The first electric line (from Stratford to Abbey Arms via Plaistow) opened on 27th February, 1904. The system embraced such populous centres as Canning Town, Forest Gate, and Stratford: particularly heavy traffic developed in connection with the West Ham football crowds: sometimes the tramway was called upon to move 20,000 people in half an hour. In 1932 the West Ham's route mileage was 16.27 miles, with its extremities at the Victoria and Albert Docks, Thatched House (Leyton Boundary), Wanstead Flats, Bow Bridge and Canning Town.

The first 100 cars, delivered by the end of 1906, were four-wheelers similar to those in general use, with Brush or M&G trucks; one exception was No. 51, which was built on a Lycett & Conaty truck. Some of the Corporation's track was not suited to bogie cars, and certain docks area lines were always worked by four-wheeled cars. However, after another batch of four-wheelers in 1910, this time on Peckham trucks, two bogie cars were purchased from Hurst Nelson in 1911. Six more four-wheelers appeared in 1923/4, and then bogie cars became the standard, 35 being purchased over the years 1925–30, some of the construction taking place in the Corporation's own workshops at Greengate Street, including the last of all, No. 68 in 1931.

This poor reproduction shows a purpose-built watering car; laying dust was important at a time when not all roads were properly surfaced. It is on a simple truck with helical springs integral with the horn-plates.

Courtesy Light Railway and Tramway Journal

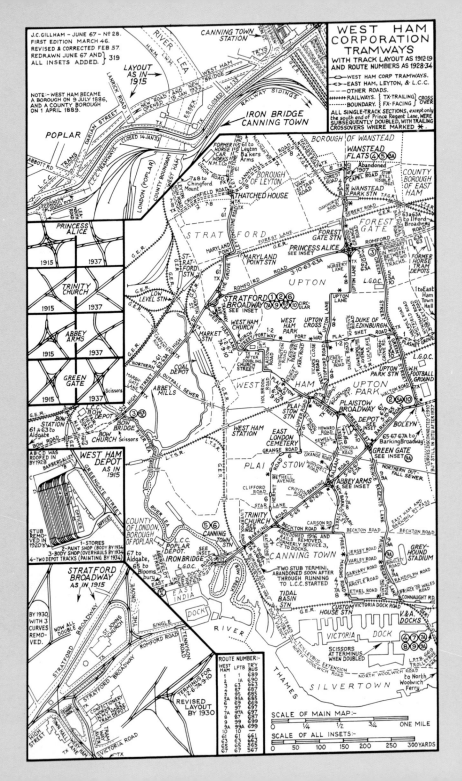

WEST HAM CORPORATION TRAMWAYS

WITH TRACK LAYOUT AS 1912-19
AND ROUTE NUMBERS AS 1928-34

J.C. GILLHAM – JUNE 67 – Nº 28.
FIRST EDITION MARCH 46.
REVISED & CORRECTED FEB 57.
REDRAWN JUNE 67 AND } 319
ALL INSETS ADDED.

NOTE:– WEST HAM BECAME
A BOROUGH ON 9 JULY 1886,
AND A COUNTY BOROUGH
ON 1 APRIL 1889.

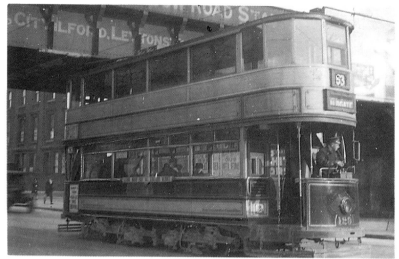

West Ham car No. 129 at Bow Road station in 1933. Seen here heading for Aldgate but travelling on LCCT track after Bow Bridge. This car is very similar to the LCC 'E1' class, built by Brush in 1929. *Author*

One of the open-topped West Ham Corporation tramcars mounted on a Brill 21E truck. The service terminated at this time at Bow Bridge. *Author's Collection*

East Ham No. 50 at Royal Albert Dock in 1932; this is on a short extension laid in 1903 to the original 1901 line. The car was built by Dick Kerr and mounted on Brill 21E truck.   *Author*

A commercial postcard showing the tram terminus at Wanstead Flats which was a short spur off the route from Forest Gate to join the Leyton line. The West Ham car is one of a batch built in 1905 by Brush equipped with Mountain & Gibson trucks.   *Lens of Sutton*

Tram Terminus, Wanstead Flats, Forest Gate. E.

The pre-War bogie cars were somewhat old-fashioned in appearance, having eight small windows to the saloon, and open ends to the top decks. West Ham cars were unusual in having their destination indicators at the top-deck roof level, and fleet numbers below the headlight.

The Corporation was seriously tempted by the Cedes-Stoll trolleybus salesmen in 1911; a single-deck car was tried out for a time, but the decision was not to buy. The car itself went on to be purchased by the Keighley Tramways, which operated Cedes-Stoll trolleys from 1913 to 1931.

ROLLING STOCK SUMMARY

Numbers	Date	Wheels	Seats	Body	Trucks	Motors
1–50	1904	4	56	Milnes	Brush	2 × 25 hp
51	1905	4	60 (as built)	Brush	Conaty radial	2 × 25 hp
52–85	1905	4	60 (as built)	Brush	M&G	2 × 25 hp
86–93	1906	4 ⎱	58–	Milnes-Voss	M&G radial	2 × 30 hp
94–100	1906	4 ⎰	62			
101–106	1910	4	58 (as built)	United Electric	Peckham	2 × 35 hp
107–118	1911	8	78 (later 74)	Nurst Nelson	Hurst Nelson	2 × 40 hp
119 & 60–63/5	1923–4	4	60	W. Ham Corp.	Peckham	2 × 35 hp
119–124	1925	8	78	Eng. Elec.	Hurst Nelson	2 × 50 hp
125–127	1925	8	69	W. Ham Corp.	H.N.	2 × 50 hp
128–137	1926	8	69	Brush	H.N.	2 × 50 hp
138	1928	8	69	W. Ham Corp.	H.N.	2 × 50 hp
81–85	1929	8	69	Brush	H.N.	2 × 50 hp
69–80	1929–30	8	73	Brush	H.N.	2 × 50 hp
68	1931			W. Ham Corp.		

Car 51 originally was fitted with the Raworth regenerative system, but was rebuilt to standard. Nos. 52–9 were entirely reconstructed in 1922. Nos. 38 and 11 were also rebuilt. The 128–137 series was re-motored and re-trucked in 1946–7. Nos. 1–93 were originally open-top, Nos. 94–118 balconied covered top, No. 119 onwards vestibuled top. Most open-tops were later covered. Car 119 was later renumbered 64 when the bogie cars came in.

All cars which had not been top-covered had gone by 1931. The Corporation had planned 11 more 4-wheeled cars for 1932/3, but the LPTB did not require them. The livery for West Ham was maroon and cream.

COUNTY BOROUGH OF EAST HAM

The East Ham undertaking was opened on 22nd June, 1901, with electric services from Manor Park Broadway to the Beckton road, and along the Barking and Romford roads. This was the second earliest electric system in London, and was considered worth a full-scale article in the USA's *Street Railway Journal*. The total mileage was only 8.34, extending to the Royal Albert Docks, Green Street and Wanstead Park.

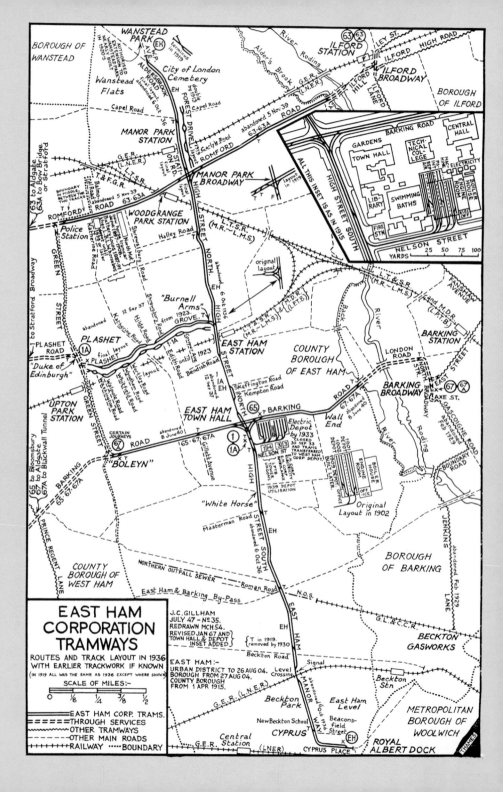

EAST HAM
CORPORATION
TRAMWAYS

ROUTES AND TRACK LAYOUT IN 1936
WITH EARLIER TRACKWORK IF KNOWN
(IN 1919 ALL WAS THE SAME AS 1936 EXCEPT WHERE SHOWN)

SCALE OF MILES:-

0   ⅛   ¼   ⅜   ½

━━━━━ EAST HAM CORP. TRAMS.
═════ THROUGH SERVICES
━━━━━ OTHER TRAMWAYS
╌╌╌╌╌ OTHER MAIN ROADS
╶╴╶╴ OTHER MAIN ROADS
+++++ RAILWAY ••••• BOUNDARY

J.C.GILLHAM
JULY 47 - No 35.
REDRAWN MCH 54.
REVISED JAN 67 AND
TOWN HALL & DEPOT
INSET ADDED.

EAST HAM:-
URBAN DISTRICT TO 26 AUG 04.
BOROUGH FROM 27 AUG 04.
COUNTY BOROUGH
FROM 1 APR 1915.

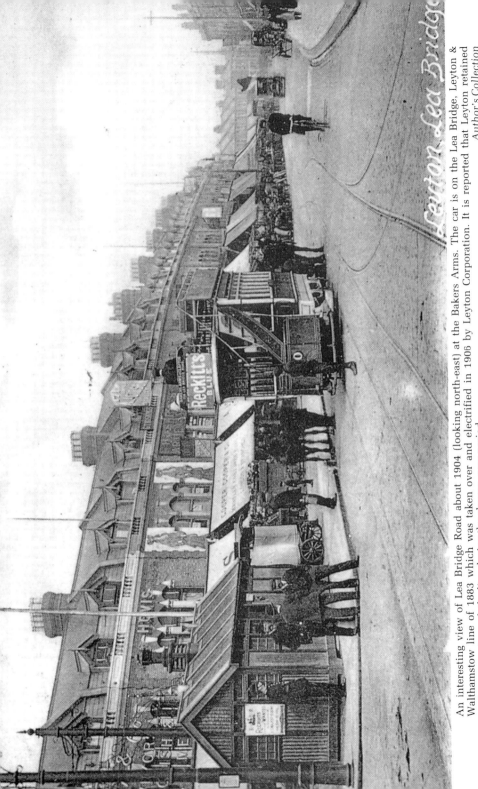

Leyton, Lea Bridge

An interesting view of Lea Bridge Road about 1904 (looking north-east) at the Bakers Arms. The car is on the Lea Bridge, Leyton & Walthamstow line of 1883 which was taken over and electrified in 1906 by Leyton Corporation. It is reported that Leyton retained ten horse-cars to work the line during the change-over period.

Author's Collection

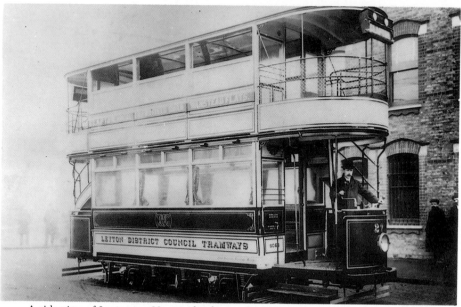

A side view of Leyton car No. 27, displaying the LUDC monogram on the side panel seen on the Clapton to Wanstead Flats route. It was built with open top in 1906, on Mountain & Gibson truck.   *Lens of Sutton*

Said to be the first car from Walthamstow to Bakers Arms on 3rd June, 1905 is Walthamstow car No. 5, with body and truck by Brush, seen here at the Bakers Arms junction. Behind the far-end of the top deck can be seen a Leyton horse-car. That line, which joined the Walthamstow one here, was to be electrified in the following year.   *Author's Collection*

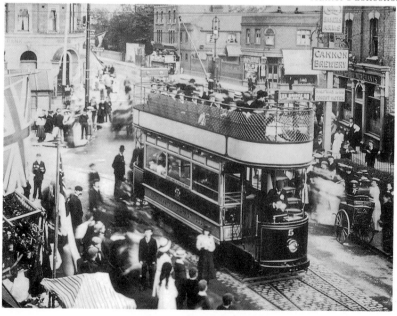

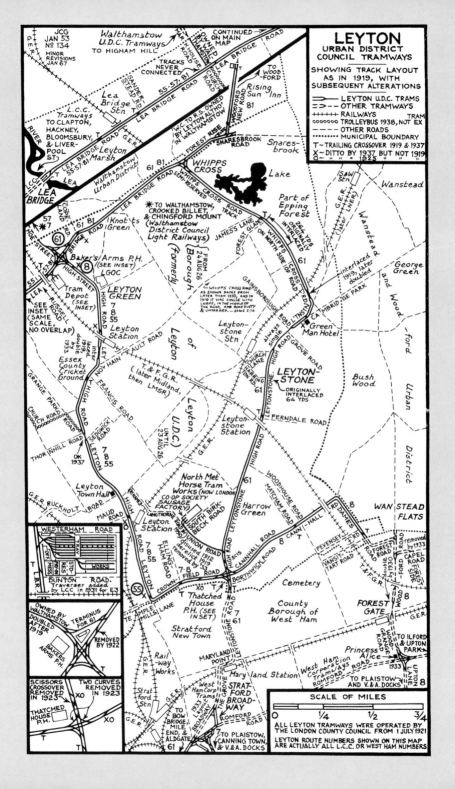

LEYTON
URBAN DISTRICT COUNCIL TRAMWAYS

SHOWING TRACK LAYOUT
AS IN 1919, WITH
SUBSEQUENT ALTERATIONS

══════	LEYTON U.D.C. TRAMS
═ ═ ═	OTHER TRAMWAYS
++++++	RAILWAYS
○○○○○○	TROLLEYBUS 1938, NOT EX TRAM
··········	OTHER ROADS
··········	MUNICIPAL BOUNDARY

T ~ TRAILING CROSSOVER 1919 & 1937
X ~ DITTO BY 1937 BUT NOT 1919
O ~ " " " 1925

SCALE OF MILES

0   ¼   ½   ¾

ALL LEYTON TRAMWAYS WERE OPERATED BY
THE LONDON COUNTY COUNCIL FROM 1 JULY 1921.
LEYTON ROUTE NUMBERS SHOWN ON THIS MAP
ARE ACTUALLY ALL L.C.C. OR WEST HAM NUMBERS

Thirty-five open-top four-wheeled cars were purchased between 1901 and 1903; eleven with covered tops came from 1905 to 1915, and then after the War a change was made to bogie cars by Brush with Brush trucks, ten in 1927 and ten in 1928; these were an improved version of the LCC 'E1' class.

The first 45 cars had round-topped roofs when top-covered, the rest flat, with open ends to the top deck, of the four-wheelers.

From 1910 East Ham cars ran over LCCT track to Aldgate, as did those of West Ham and Leyton.

ROLLING STOCK SUMMARY

Numbers	Date	Wheels	Seats	Body	Trucks	Motors
1–35	1901–3	4	56	Dick, Kerr	Brill	2 × 25 hp
36–45	1905–10	4	56	U.E.C.	Peckham	2 × 40 hp
46	1915	4	56	Brush	Peckham	2 × 40 hp
47–50	1921	4	56	Brush	Peckham	2 × 40 hp
51–70	1927–28	8	72	Brush	Brush	2 × 60 hp

BOROUGH OF LEYTON (Formerly Leyton Urban District Council)

The Leyton lines were acquired from the North Metropolitan and Lea Bridge, Leyton & Walthamstow Tramways, already mentioned. Electric traction began on 1st December, 1906, and operation was handed over to the LCCT on 1st July, 1921, although the cars remained in LUDC livery with a monogram of these letters combined on the side panel, until 1931.

All the original 4-wheelers were withdrawn in 1931–2 as new 'E3' class cars allocated by LCCT (paid for by Leyton) came into service. As only four-wheelers were allowed on the Docks route, some 'M' class cars were loaned, the fleet of 10 at Abbey Wood were fitted with ploughs and transferred in 1931 to Leyton.

ROLLING STOCK SUMMARY

Numbers	Date	Wheels	Body	Trucks	Motors
1–10	horse cars				
11–50	1906	4	Milnes Voss	M & G radial	2 × 30 hp Westinghouse
51–70	1907	4	Milnes Voss	M & G radial	2 × 30 hp Westinghouse
161–210 (LCCT numbers) 'E3' class, BTH 509 motors					2 × 60 hp

WALTHAMSTOW CORPORATION (formerly Walthamstow U.D.C.)

This system, 'Walthamstow Light Railways', comprising only three routes (8.93 miles), opened complete, with electric traction, on 3rd June, 1905. Its history was uneventful, and its rolling stock showed an orderly progression towards modernisation, the last cars being delivered not long before the undertaking's absorption in the LPTB. The extremities of the system were: Baker's Arms, Napier Arms, Chingford Mount, Higham Hill and Ferry Lane. The cars were painted brown with dull yellow lower panels.

Walthamstow No. 32, the last of the 1905 batch of Brush cars, after having a top cover fitted, at Woodford in April 1932. *Author*

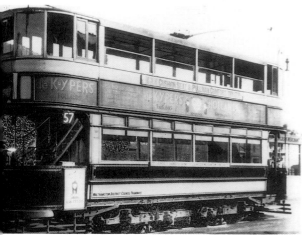

Walthamstow No. 57 was similar to the LCCT 'E1' class, and one of a dozen built by Hurst Nelson in 1927. These cars could be seen at the terminus at the east side of Liverpool Street station, and route 57 ran out to Chingford. Note the message on the side 'This car has Cushion Seats: Pullman Comfort – Try it!!'. *Lens of Sutton*

Walthamstow No. 48, one of the cars built new in 1932, running on route 2 via Hoe Street to Bakers Arms. These trams had windscreens fitted from the start. *Lens of Sutton*

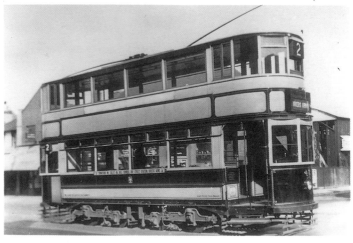

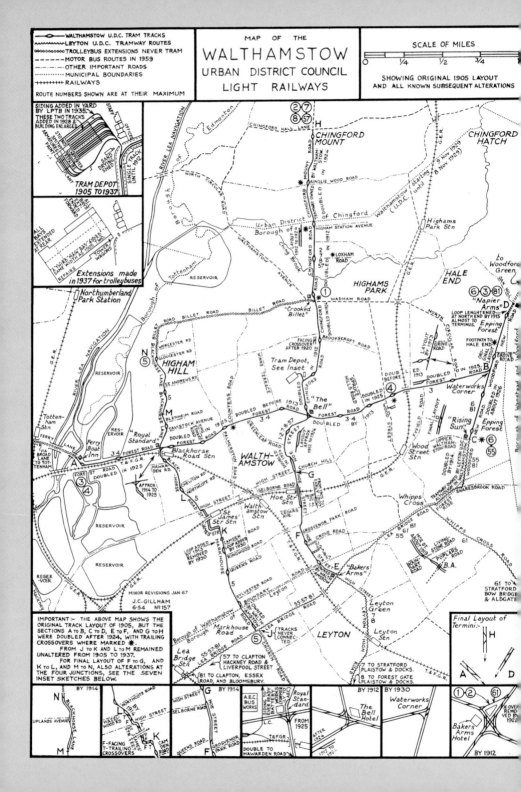

MAP OF THE
WALTHAMSTOW
URBAN DISTRICT COUNCIL
LIGHT RAILWAYS

Key:
- ⬭⬭ WALTHAMSTOW U.D.C. TRAM TRACKS
- ⋀⋀ LEYTON U.D.C. TRAMWAY ROUTES
- ∞∞∞ TROLLEYBUS EXTENSIONS NEVER TRAM
- — — MOTOR BUS ROUTES IN 1959
- — · — OTHER IMPORTANT ROADS
- — ·· — MUNICIPAL BOUNDARIES
- +++++ RAILWAYS

ROUTE NUMBERS SHOWN ARE AT THEIR MAXIMUM

SCALE OF MILES

0   ¼   ½   ¾

SHOWING ORIGINAL 1905 LAYOUT
AND ALL KNOWN SUBSEQUENT ALTERATIONS

SIDING ADDED IN YARD
BY LPTB IN 1935.
THESE TWO TRACKS
ADDED IN 1928 &
BUILDING ENLARGED

**TRAM DEPOT
1905 TO 1937**

ALL
BAYS
EXTENDED
AT REAR

Extensions made
in 1937 for trolleybuses

Northumberland
Park Station

MINOR REVISIONS JAN 67

J.C. GILLHAM
6·54   No 157

IMPORTANT:— THE ABOVE MAP SHOWS THE
ORIGINAL TRACK LAYOUT OF 1905, BUT THE
SECTIONS A TO B, C TO D, E TO F, AND G TO H
WERE DOUBLED AFTER 1924, WITH TRAILING
CROSSOVERS WHERE MARKED *.
    FROM J TO K AND L TO M REMAINED
UNALTERED FROM 1905 TO 1937.
    FOR FINAL LAYOUT OF F TO G, AND
K TO L, AND M TO N, ALSO ALTERATIONS AT
THE FOUR JUNCTIONS, SEE THE SEVEN
INSET SKETCHES BELOW.

Final Layout of
Termini:-

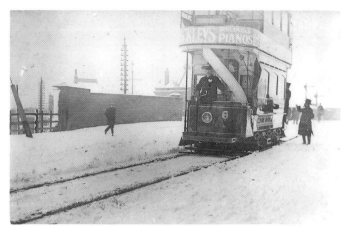

On a wintry morning in 1906, Ilford car No. 6 stops at Seven Kings station on its way down the High Road to Chadwell Heath; note the reversed stairway.   *D.E. Brewster Collection*

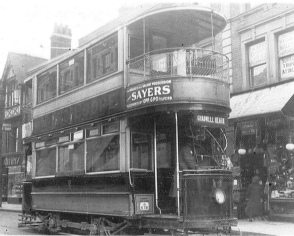

Ilford tramcar No. 14 was of a later batch built on Brush trucks and re-numbered to take the place of earlier cars; it is seen here in April 1932 at Ilford ready to return to Chadwell Heath.   *Author*

How the 'Essex Times' saw the end of Barking trams, the first of the Municipal lines to close down; from the issue of 9th March, 1929.
                    Author's Collection

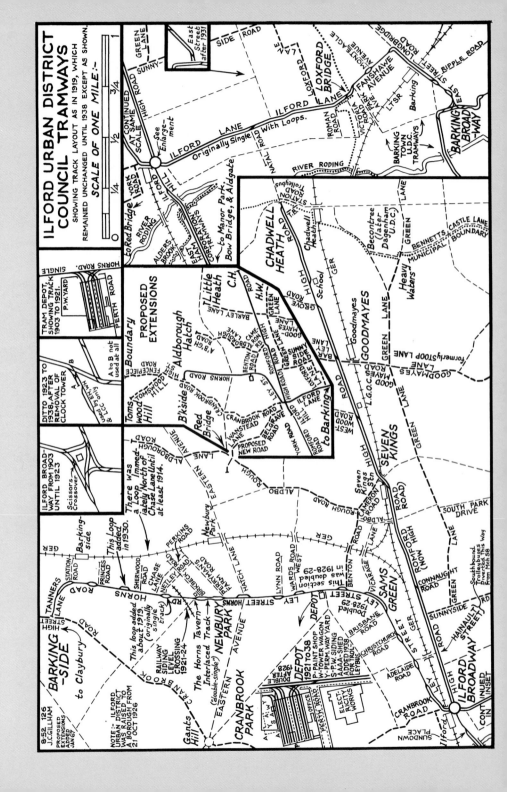

ILFORD URBAN DISTRICT COUNCIL TRAMWAYS

SHOWING TRACK LAYOUT AS IN 1919, WHICH REMAINED UNCHANGED UNTIL 1938 EXCEPT AS SHOWN.

SCALE OF ONE MILE:-

1   3/4   1/2   1/4

B-52 126
J.C.GILLHAM
PROPOSED
EXTENSIONS
Jan 67

NOTE:- ILFORD
U.D.C. WAS RAISED TO
A BOROUGH FROM
21 OCT 1926

ILFORD BROADWAY FROM 1903
UNTIL 1923
Scissors-
Crossover

DITTO 1923 TO
1938, AFTER REMOVAL OF
CLOCK TOWER
A to B not
used at all
used by ERWH
& LCC only

TRAM DEPOT, SHOWING TRACK
1903 TO 1921.
P.W.YARD
PERTH ROAD
HORNS ROAD
SINGLE

PROPOSED
EXTENSIONS

Boundary

Toms wood Hill
B'kside Road
Red Bridge
TOMSWOOD HILL
HIGH ROAD
FENCEPIECE ROAD
ALDBOROUGH ROAD

There was
a Loop immed-
iabely North of
Chase Lane Until
at least 1914.

Little Heath
Aldborough Hatch
C.H.

BARLEY LANE

CHADWELL HEATH

Becontree
(later
Dagenham
U.D.C.)

BENNETTS CASTLE LANE

MUNICIPAL BOUNDARY

Heavy
Waters

GOODMAYES

GREEN LANE

formerly STOOP LANE

SEVEN KINGS

SOUTH PARK DRIVE

ROMFORD ROAD (NOW A.12 ROAD)

Southbound
Trolleybuses
Travel this Way
From Mch 38

CONNAUGHT ROAD
SUNNYSIDE
HAINAULT STREET
ADELAIDE ROAD

ILFORD BROADWAY

BARKING SIDE
to Claybury

This Loop
added in 1930.

This loop added
about 1919,
(originally
single
single track

The Horns Tavern
Interlaced Track
(double-single)

RAILWAY
SIDING
LEVEL
CROSSING
1921-24

NEWBURY PARK

CRANBROOK PARK

EASTERN AVENUE

DEPOT
1921 TO 38
P-PAINT SHOP
A-S-P.W.YARD
S-P.W. SIDING
A-A-A-SHED
ADDED 1938
FOR TROL-
LEYBUS
DOUBLE
1928

ELECT-
RICITY
WORKS

OFFICE

This section
Doubled
in 1928-29

Doubled
1928-29

Southbound

to Barking

ILFORD LANE
Originally Single With Loops.

See Enlarge-
ment

CAT continued AT SAME SCALE NOW

GREEN LANE
SIDE ROAD
SUNNY
HIGH ROAD
East
Street
after 1931

LOXFORD BRIDGE

FANSHAWE AVENUE

VICTORIA RD

ROMAN ROAD

BARKING TOWN
U.D.C. TRAMWAYS

BARKING BROADWAY

RIVER RODING

to Manor Park
Bow Bridge, & Aldgate

CHADWELL HEATH STATION Trolleybus

School

GROVE ROAD

GOODMAYES LANE

to Barking

Seven Kings Stn

BARKINGSIDE

to Red Bridge
RIVER RODING
ALDERS BROOK
EAST HAM CORPORATION TRAMWAYS

Proposed
New Road
WANSTEAD
CRANBROOK ROAD
BELGRAVE ROAD
YORK ROAD
ROMFORD ROAD
ALDBOROUGH

HIGH ROAD
HORNS ROAD
BENTON ROAD
HIGH ROAD
SUNNY SIDE LANE
LEY ST.
TIBBORO HIGH
GREEN LANE
ILFORD LANE

STATION ROAD
PRINCES ROAD
SHERWOOD ROAD
CHASE LANE
BIRBECK ROAD
NETLEY ROAD
PERKINS ROAD

PERTH ROAD
HORNS ROAD

LYNN ROAD
WARDS ROAD
BRISBANE ROAD
BENTON ROAD
VICARAGE LANE
CHRISTCHURCH ROAD

STREET
LEY STREET
SAMS GREEN

ROMFORD HIGH
STREET

CRANBROOK ROAD
SUNDOWN PLACE
CONTINUED AFTER

Newbury Park

EASTERN
AVENUE

TANNERS LANE
HIGH STREET
BROOK ROAD

Gants Hill

ROLLING STOCK SUMMARY

Numbers	Date	Wheels	Seats	Body	Trucks	Motors
1–32	1905	4	52	Brush	Brush	2 × 25 hp
33–38	1911	4	56	Hurst Nelson	Hurst Nelson	2 × 30 hp
(39–46)	1919	8	36*	E.R.T.C.W.	Brill	4 × 25 hp
47–52	1920	8	69	British Elec.	Brill	2 × 25 hp
53–64	1927	8	69	Hurst Nelson	Hurst Nelson	2 × 63 hp
39–46	1932	8	69	Brush	Brush P35	2 × 63 hp

*The original Nos. 39–46 were single-deck, and were withdrawn by 1931; the replacement cars were similar to LCCT 'E3' cars.

BOROUGH OF ILFORD (formerly Ilford Urban District Council)

The 7.13 miles of this undertaking were opened in March 1903; the line ran from Ilford to Chadwell Heath and Barkingside, and a junction with the Barking tramways at Loxford Bridge was effected in 1905. Connection was made at Ilford Bridge with the East Ham lines.

ROLLING STOCK SUMMARY

Numbers	Date	Wheels	Seats	Body	Trucks	Motors
1–12	1903	4	57	Hurst Nelson	Hurst Nelson	2 × 25 hp
13–18	1903	8	69	Hurst Nelson	Hurst Nelson	2 × 30 hp
19–22	1903	4	57	Hurst Nelson	Hurst Nelson	2 × 25 hp
23–26	1909	4	?	Brush	Brush	2 × 25 hp
27–28	1914	4	?	Brush	Brush	2 × 25 hp
1–23	1920–30	4	?	Brush	Brush	2 × 25 hp
33–40	1932	4	68	Brush	Brush	4 × 40 hp

Nos. 27/8 were ex-Barking cars.

The bogie cars were converted in 1923 to four-wheelers on Ilford long-wheelbase trucks, and these trucks were later fitted also to the second batch. The last batch of eight cars were sold to Sunderland Corporation. In 1914 two cars were obtained from the Barking Council. The livery was red (later green) and cream. Most 1903–09 cars were renumbered at least once, some twice.

The 1932 cars had no windshields, as the General Manager considered open platforms to be healthier.

BARKING TOWN LIGHT RAILWAY (formerly Barking U.D.C.)

Service was begun on 15th December, 1903, between Gascoigne Road and Beckton Gas Works. Part of the Barking system was always worked by Ilford, and operation by Barking U.D.C. ceased in February 1929, when the Beckton route was abandoned and East Ham took over the remainder. The connection with Ilford was at Loxford Bridge.

The original stock was seven Brush four-wheel open-top cars, with reversed stairs; some were covered and fitted with normal stairs later. The stock figure rose to nine during the year prior to World War I, but declined to six by February 1929. Two cars were sold to Ilford in 1914.

Barking cars were distinguished by having a diamond border around the number on the front shield.

CITY OF LONDON

The Blackfriars Bridge Tramway, opened on 14th September, 1909, was operated under lease by LCCT.

HERTFORDSHIRE COUNTY COUNCIL

A line from the County boundary south of Long Street to Barnet was opened on 28th March, 1907; and from Freezy Water to Waltham Cross on 17th April, 1908; both lines were leased to MET.

MIDDLESEX COUNTY COUNCIL

All lines in the northern half of the County were leased to MET; however for a time certain types of car carried 'County Council of Middlesex' on their lower side panels.

Left: Barking car No. 8 at Loxford Bridge, Barking, on the Ilford Boundary to Poplar route; an early Ilford car with reversed stairway can be seen in the background. The areas of the East London boroughs were so small that some inter-running was a necessity.
Lens of Sutton

Right: A signal placed to warn drivers of East Ham trams if the level-crossing gates for the LNER branch railway to Beckton were against them. It was photographed in 1933.   *Autho*

Chapter Nine
Under London Transport

The Bill to nationalise London transport had been a political football for several years in a period of bad Government, and was forced through in 1933 by Herbert Morrison, Minister of Transport in the 1929 Parliament, with the connivance of Lord Ashfield, head of the Underground Group, which owned all the underground railways, almost all the buses, but only a quarter of the trams. The London Passenger Transport Board, which assumed power on 1st July, 1933, worked out of the former 'Company' head office at Broadway, Westminster, and it was fairly obvious what would happen. The 'Company' had already started with trolleybuses and was about to put on the streets the first reliable oil-engined bus, the STL. Trams would be run down; trolleybuses would be put on to use the capital value of the power transmissions systems, but in the end the bus would win. The value of the trolleybus interlude, which lasted 30 years, has been questioned; it might have been better to run the trams longer and to switch straight to buses. Anyway, rules were bent for the trolleys; overhead was put up in Central London street where tram owners had been forbidden to do so; turning circles for the buses (which of course were not reversible), were made at some inconvenience to other traffic.

A total of 1891 trolleybuses was obtained, of many differing classes; the last order was for 50 of class Q1 in 1952.

Meanwhile, the Board had 2,630 tramcars on its books, which could not be run down quickly. The first thing was to apply letter keys to the stock of the smaller systems, which might become confused as many of the four-wheelers looked similar. These letters, which appeared on the right of the number, were C for Bexley; D, Erith; E, Croydon; F, Ilford; G, East Ham; H, West Ham; K, Walthamstow; S, Southmet. Leyton cars already carried LCCT numbers.

The first systems scheduled to be converted to trolleybus operation were the Bexley & Dartford. Erith, SMET, Walthamstow, Ilford and LUT. It was felt that the cars of the first two should not continue to be used, even for a brief time, so before the end of the year 49 LCCT 'M' class cars with plough gear removed were sent to Bexley, to handle the area, including Erith, as a group. Some of the four-wheeled Erith cars were rebuilt on Brill 21E trucks from Croydon cars and allowed to work until 1935, when trolleybuses took over; they worked in London Transport red and cream livery but bearing their former Erith numbers, as no LPTB fleet numbers were allotted to Erith. However, Erith No. 8's truck was put under a West Ham car (LPTB No. 58).

Other cars which were sent to Bexley included Croydon No. 5, running as LPTB 349, and East Ham Nos. 21 and 27 (LPTB 53/8).

From 1936 conversion work switched to north and east London, and as a result some strange cars found themselves south of the river. The 20 East Ham cars 51–70 were very similar in appearance to the 'E1' class, and four which were moved to Abbey Wood attracted little attention; the remainder were stored at Hampstead depot, but were needed later during the War. West Ham cars Nos. 68–85 and 125–138 were also not unlike the 'E1s', though their electrical equipment was very different, and when they came south

This ex-MET type 'A' tramcar, running as LPTB No. 2421 was one of the Board's oldest vehicles (and looked the part). Again the adverts are very interesting.

London Transport

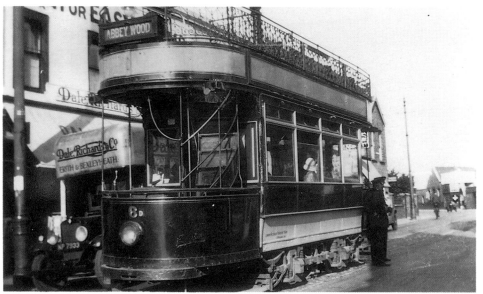

Open top Erith tramcar No. 6 *en-route* to Abbey Wood did not carry its 'D' suffix for long; seen here in Bexleyheath Market Place *c.*1934.   *Lens of Sutton*

A 'E3' class double deck car trundles up the incline to Westminster Bridge past Boadicea's statue in 1947 on route 40.   *Author*

The LPTB phased out the Bexley cars quickly; here ex-LCCT 'M' class No. 1705 is seen at the Bexleyheath depot in July 1933. A total of 49 'M' class covered Bexley and Erith routes, but in 1935 trolleybuses took over. *London Transport*

This very interesting side view of a class 'E1' car was circulated to advertising agencies in 1934 to sell the advertising spaces, particularly the 'dashboard' area. *London Transport*

they had the plough carriers removed from one bogie to the frame, as had progressively been done with the 'E1' class itself.

The Ilford system, which is said to have been the only 'borough' line to show a consistent profit (and also the only one on which LCCT all-day tour tickets were not valid) lasted until 1938, all 40 received board numbers, 5 to 44.

The LCCT had in 1932 experimented with rebuilding some 'E1' cars with metal flush sides, covering the previously exposed sole-bar, and a few cars were also given domed roofs in 1934. In 1935 the Board began a programme of 'rehabilitating' 'E1' cars (and a few others) which included flush-siding, better upholstery, and windscreens. This programme was discontinued in the following year, although most cars which came in for overhaul were given windscreens. Cars were also re-rostered so that on the whole cars without windscreens were concentrated in certain depots.

By the time War broke out in 1939 the only tram routes left north of the river were from Aldgate to Barking (converted 9th June, 1940) and Aldgate to Ilford and to Leyton, which went on 5th November, 1939; there were also the Kingsway Tunnel routes running north to Hackney, Manor House and Archway, and Moorgate to Highgate Hill.

The Board had already begun to sell some of its best cars; three 'HR2' class went to Leeds in 1939, while one of the experimental Felthams, MET No. 331, was sold to Sunderland in 1938 (and preserved when that system closed in 1954). In the same year Ilford Cars now LPTB Nos. 33–40 were sold to Sunderland.

The Second World War was to have a heavy impact on the tramways. For one thing, they were much harder to work in the blackout; the headlights on the cars were shielded and converted to be useable as rear-lights; this improvement was left in place afterwards. Then there was the damage to the track; re-erecting trolley wires was no great problem, but twisted conduit was another matter. As regards the cars, 69 trams were recorded as totally destroyed; this included a number of the most modern LCCT cars: Nos. 1852/3/65/89/99/1900/1/2/3. Abbey Wood depot was bombed in 1941, but at that time only housed former West Ham cars; No. 303 was lost and possibly others. Far more serious was the bomb on Camberwell depot which destroyed 20 trams.

Meanwhile the Feltham cars had come south, and were much appreciated by travellers whose only luxury tram had previously been No. 1. There were some routes where their great overhang made them inadmissable.

After the War, the Board reviewed the situation several times and in 1946 made a definite decision to phase out both trams and trolleybuses in favour of oil-engined buses, by this time mainly by STL. However, the implementation had to be put off; there was an unprecedented shortage of buses at the time, causing the Board to hire all sorts of coaches to boost peak hours capacity, and to take on a number of buses in the liveries of other cities. By 1948, when the Board gave way to the London Transport Executive, there were 830 trams left, running on 102 miles of route. Some of these were 'E1' cars with bracing straps diagonally across the sides of the bodies, which were by now showing movement.

One of the 'Feltham' cars sold to Leeds City, their No. 501. Note that it has been fitted with a bow current collector; bows were tested in London but not adopted.

AEL Ltd

Leyton 'E3' class No. 189, one of a batch ordered for the Council by the LCCT in its last years, leaves Bakers Arms junction to run via Lea Bridge Road, Whipps Cross and Leytonstone to the Aldgate terminus, about 1935. *Lens of Sutton*

The first bus replacement was on 1st October, 1950 and continued as a rolling programme until 5th July, 1952, at the end of a well-publicised 'Last Tram Week'. Meanwhile in 1951, ninety Feltham cars had been sold to Leeds City Tramways.

The last tram ran from Woolwich to New Cross Depot just after midnight on 5th/6th July. A contract had been let to the firm of George Cohen to scrap the remaining trams on a field near Charlton Football Ground.

Fortunately a number of trams have been preserved for posterity (see Appendix 2). What posterity will never know is the joy of settling down in the front seat at the top of an 'E1' at Westminster Pier for a fascinating run out to Eltham, for the sum of 2d. (1p).

Of course, at the time of its demise the London tram was already an anachronism: a vehicle which deposited its passengers in the middle of the road, and announced its progress by clanging a bell like a muffin-man. The trouble was that the councils, historically wedded to low fares, never had the money to improve their lines or cars, and the Company was more interested in its buses and trains. Once the whole lot got into the hands of a body whose senior management was opposed to tramways, there could be only one answer. It is also probably true that tramways had to spend much more on maintaining their track than the buses paid for their licences. However, Continental cities make it work, in many cases by not having buses, and manage plenty of reserved setting-down areas. Had London started to change early enough, it could have been done here. The Docklands Light Railway and Manchester have shown that the tram is not dead; many other Light Railways are being planned in various towns. The ring of metal wheel on metal rail is always satisfactory; a Docklands car may not please the enthusiast as much as an old LUT 'U'-type, but it is better than nothing.

A congested scene in Woolwich High Street on 5th July, 1952 (the last tram working day). *Left to right* are class 'E3', No. 1916; ex-West Ham No. 309 (a type similar to the class 'E1') and type 'D2' trolleybus No. 442.   *D.E. Brewster Collection*

Appendix One

LPTB Stock Numbers:
Conversion From Former Numbers, 1933

LPTB No.	Former No.	Former Owner	Type
1	1	LCC	HR2 Mod.
2	—	LPTB	E/1 Reb.
5–32	1–28	Ilford	
33–40	33–40	"	1932 series
41–44	29–32	"	Oldest cars
45–80	1–50*	E. Ham	4-wheel
81–100	51–70	"	Bogie
101–160	101–160	LCC	HR2
161–210	161–210	Leyton	E/3
211–258	1–50*	W. Ham	4-wheel
259–273	51–65	"	"
274–294	86–106	"	"
295–344	68–85, 107–138	"	Bogie
345–364	1–20	Croydon	W/1
365–374	21–30	"	B/2
375–399	31–55	"	Bogie
402–551	Same	LCC	E
552–601	"	"	E/1
602–751	"	"	E
752–1426	"	"	E/1
1427–1476	"	"	M
1477–1676	"	"	E/1
1677–1726	"	"	M
1727–1851	"	"	E/1
1852	"	"	HR1
1853	"	"	HR2 non-std.
1854–1903	"	"	HR2
1904–2003	"	"	E/3
2004–2041	1–38†	Walthamstow	4-wheel
2042–2053	51–62	"	Bogie
2054–2061	39–46	"	"
2062–5	47–50	"	s.d.
2066–2119	319, 321–329, 332–375	MET	UCC
2120–2165	351–396	LUT	UCC
2166	320	MET	Experimental
2167/8	330/1	"	"
2169–2254	237–314, 316, 2, 12, 22, 31, 46, 82 & 315	MET	H
2255	318	"	Bluebell
2256–60	212–216	"	F
2261	317	"	G mod.
2262–81	217–236	"	G
2282–2301	192–211	"	C1
2302–2316	131–150*	"	E
2317	350	LUT	Poppy
2318–2357	301–340‡	"	T
2358–2402	151–300*	"	U

LPTB No.	Former No.	Former Owner	Type
2403–5	155, 199, 288	"	U2
2406–2410	157, 161, 211, 243 & 261	"	WT
2411	247	"	UX
2412–2466	71–130*†	MET	A
2467–2482	1–70*	"	B2
2483–2497	151–165	"	C2
2498–2521	1–70*	"	B
2522–2529	151–300	LUT	W

*Not complete series; survivors only.
†Not renumbered in correct sequence.
‡307 became 2357, not 2324; otherwise renumbered in order.

Between 1936 and 1938 a number of 'E1' class cars had their numbers exchanged in order to group together those which had their motors replaced with high-power motors and those which retained the original low-power motors. However, 17 cars with numbers under 1000 were still in service in 1939 in addition to the 552–601 series, and the West Ham & East Ham bogie cars, and the new cars 101–210.

Appendix Two
Preserved Trams

The realisation that examples of tramcars should be preserved for future generations to see came too late to save examples of most early types, though one or two survived by accident. The following is believed to be the present location of preserved cars.

The London Transport Museum, formerly in Clapham tram shed but now at Covent Garden, contains MET 'Feltham' car 355, LCCT 'E1' No. 1025, West Ham No. 290, ex-West Ham 102 and Stephenson horse-car No. 284 from the London Tramways Co.

The National Tramway Museum at Crich has: the MET experimental car 331, which had been sold to Sunderland, but returned; LCCT 'B' class No. 106, LCCT 'special' No. 1, London Street Tramways horse-car No. 39, parts of a North Metropolitan horse-car, and an LUT lower saloon.

The LCC Tramways Trust has an 'E1' (1622) being rebuilt.

East Anglia Transport Museum, LCCT 'HR2' No. 1858 and a dismantled LCCT trailer.

Caister Castle Motor Museum; a horse car of the London Southern Tramways.

Seashore Electric Railway, USA: LPTB Feltham car 2085. This had later been Leeds City No. 526; the railway is at Kennebunkport, Maine.

Howth Castle Transport Museum, Dublin: LCCT trailer No. T24.

Seaton & District Tramway: running on this 2 ft 9 in. gauge electric tramway is the narrowed body of MET No. 94, as single-decker 14.

Oxford Bus Museum, Long Hanborough, has ex-North Metropolitan horse-car 707 (which was sold to the Oxford tramways), to be restored in Oxford livery.

(The above information kindly supplied by J.H. Price, National Tramway Museum.)

Appendix Three

Starting Dates of the Main LCC Electric Routes

14th October, 1903	Cable Depot, Kennington–City Termini
21st May, 1904	Cable Depot–Brixton Station
30th May, 1904	Brixton Station–Water Lane, Brixton
19th June, 1904	Water Lane–Streatham
31st July, 1909	Streatham–Norbury
5th November, 1910	Mitcham Road–Streatham High Road via Mitcham Lane

4th April, 1908	Vauxhall–Brixton Road via South Lambeth Road
21st November, 1908	Brixton Road–Denmark Hill via Loughborough Junction
28th May, 1909	Loughborough Junction–Herne Hill Station
30th May, 1909	Herne Hill Station–Norwood
5th April, 1912	Brixton Road–Herne Hill via Effra Road and Dulwich Rd

15th May, 1903	Waterloo Station Blackfriars Bridge (South side) } to Tooting High Street Westminster Bridge (South side) } via Clapham
6th August, 1905	Tooting High Street–Tooting Broadway
13th October, 1907	Tooting Broadway–Merton (County Boundary)
2nd May, 1922	Through service to Wimbledon via Clapham, Tooting and Colliers Wood

25th June, 1903	Camberwell–Kennington via Camberwell New Road
2nd August, 1903	Kennington–Vauxhall via Harleyford Road
5th August, 1906	Vauxhall–Victoria Station via Vauxhall Bridge

5th August, 1906	Tooting Broadway–Plough Road, Battersea via Garratt Lane
13th October, 1906	Plough Road–Queens Road, Battersea Clapham Junction–Battersea via Falcon Road
22nd December, 1906	Queen's Road, Battersea–Vauxhall via Battersea Park Road
8th September, 1906	Vauxhall–St. Thomas's Hospital via Albert Embankment
24th September, 1906	Lambeth Road–Hop Exchange
15th December, 1906	Embankment Tramways–Blackfriars
14th September, 1909	Blackfriars Bridge
25th January, 1909	Chelsea Bridge–Lavender Hill via Queens Road
26th February, 1910	Lavender Hill (Cedars Road)–Plough, Clapham via Long Road, Clapham Common

23rd September, 1909	Nine Elms Lane–Cedars Road via Wandsworth Road
9th October, 1909	Cedars Road, Clapham–Clapham Junction via Lavender Hill
16th December, 1909	Clapham Junction–East Hill

22nd June, 1911	Battersea Park Road–King's Road, Chelsea

30th May, 1908	Hammersmith–Harlesden
23rd January, 1909	Putney–Hammersmith
30th January, 1912	Putney–Wandsworth
16th July, 1915	High Street, Wandsworth

17th January, 1904	Elephant & Castle–New Cross and Deptford
30th January, 1906	New Cross Gate–Lewisham Obelisk
10th June, 1906	Lewisham Obelisk–Rushey Green
18th June, 1906	Woolwich–Blackwall Tunnel
4th May, 1907	Lewisham Obelisk–Lee Green

4th April, 1908	South St. Greenwich–Lewisham Obelisk
17th April, 1908	Woolwich Beresford Sq.–Plumstead Ch.
26th July, 1908	Plumstead Church–Abbey Wood
26th February, 1909	Lewisham High Rd.–Brockley Lane Stn
23rd July, 1910	Woolwich–Eltham Church via Well Hall Road
5th August, 1911	Creek Bridge–Greenwich Church
28th November, 1912	Tooley St.–Stanier St.
9th December, 1912	Tooley St.–Duke St.
5th April, 1914	Woolwich Church St–Nile St.
29th November, 1920	Lee Green–Eltham Lyme Farm
22nd March, 1921	Lyme Farm–Eltham Church
14th July, 1925	Across Southwark Bridge
28th September, 1926	Southend Villege–Downham
28th July, 1927	Downham–Southover
15th November, 1931	Eltham Well Hall Rd.–Westhorne Ave.
30th June, 1932	Briset Rd.–'Yorkshire Grey' Eltham

Appendix Four

Metropolitan Electric Tramways: Dates of Opening

22nd July, 1904	Finsbury Park to Wood Green
	Manor House to Edmonton (1st section Seven Sisters Corner)
20th August, 1904	Bruce Grove to Lordship Lane
3rd December, 1904	Edgware Road to Church Lane
12th April, 1905	Stamford Hill to Seven Sisters Corner
	Manor House to Edmonton (2nd section Edmonton boundary)
7th June, 1905	Great North Road to Oakleigh Road
19th July, 1905	Manor House to Edmonton (3rd section Tramway Avenue)
24th August, 1905	Manor House to Edmonton (4th section)
6th December, 1905	Turnpike Lane to Muswell Hill
	Priory Road to Alexandra Palace
22nd December, 1905	Archway Tavern to Highgate Archway
31st March, 1906	Cricklewood Lane to Craven Park
	Chichele Road to Cricklewood Lane
30th April, 1906	Wood Green to Alexandra Palace
4th August, 1906	Totteridge Lane to County Boundary
10th October, 1906	High Street, Harlesden to Wembley (Iron Bridge)
28th November, 1906	Lordship Lane to Ranelagh P.H.
22nd December, 1906	Royal Oak, Harlesden, to Lock Bridge
29th March, 1907	County Boundary to Barnet Terminus
11th May, 1907	Ranelagh P.H. to Southgate
7th June, 1907	Kings Arms Bridge to Wood Green (Green Lanes)
1st August, 1907	Winchmore Hill to Kings Arms Bridge
31st October, 1907	Edgware to Canons Park
11th December, 1907	Tramway Avenue to County Boundary
23rd December, 1907	Willesden Green Station to Craven Park

15th April, 1908	Iron Bridge to Wembley
17th April, 1908	County Boundary to Waltham Cross
3rd June, 1908	Jubilee Clock (Harlesden) to Willesden Junction
8th April, 1909	Station Road, New Southgate to Great North Road, Finchley
3rd July, 1909	Green Dragon Hotel to Enfield Town
8th October, 1909	Horn Lane, Acton, to Station Road, Harlesden
17th December, 1909	Golders Green to North Finchley
22nd February, 1910	Golders Green to Cricklewood Terminus
14th July, 1910	Lock Bridge to Warwick Crescent
6th December, 1910	Warwick Crescent to Edgware Road
20th February, 1911	Hertford Road to Enfield Town
1st August, 1912	Finsbury Park–Manor House taken over by LCC

Bibliography

Considerable use has been made in compiling this booklet of the files of *The Engineer, Engineering, The Omnibus Magazine*, the New York *Street Car Journal, Tramway and Light Railway News*, and other periodicals; also Dr H.A. Whitcombe: *proc. Inst. Loco. Eng.*, 1937, No. 327 (The History of the Steam Tram); D.K. Clark: Tramways, Their Construction and Working, 1878 and 1894; J.A. Brill, The Development of the Tramcar: *Cassiers Magazine*, XVI, No. 369. Special Supplements published by *The Omnibus Magazine* in 1932 covering the LUT and MET systems have been most valuable.

The following books which have come out since the first edition was published are recommended for more detailed information on certain subjects: *London Transport* in two vols. by T.C. Barker & R. Michael Robbins, (Allen & Unwin 1974) for financial and political backgrounds to tramways in London over their whole history; *London County Council Tramway Handbook* by 'Kennington', Tramway & Light Railway Society 1970, for information on routes, cars and track-work; *The Tramways of Woolwich and South East London* by 'Southeastern', Light Railway Transport League 1963, for detailed history of all tramways and cars using them from Woolwich to Horns Cross; *Improving London's Trams 1932–7* for the full story of upgrading the 'E1' class, Oakley & Withey, Light Railway Transport League; *The Tramways of Croydon*, G.E. Baddeley, Light Railway Transport League 1983.

Acknowledgments

Amongst those who assisted with the first edition of this book, grateful thanks must go to D.W.K. Jones for much of the rolling stock information. The London Transport information officers were very helpful in supplying photographs, not then easily found, to supplement the author's own. Since then, many people have written with helpful amendments and additions, including G.H. Cannon, Eric Fayne, J.H. Price, D.G. Mumby, Robert Eastleigh, R.H. Hiscock, and D.E. Brewster and last of all my deepest thanks to John C. Gillham for his detailed checking and additions.